Chemistry

Revision Notes

Author
Rob Ritchie

Series editor
Alan Brewerton

A level

EDUCATIONAL

Every effort has been made to trace copyright holders and to obtain their permission for the use of copyright material. The authors and publishers will glady receive information enabling them to rectify any error or omission in subsequent editions.

First published 1998

Letts Educational Schools and Colleges Division, 9–15 Aldine Street, London W12 8AW
Tel. 0181 740 2270
Fax 0181 740 2280

Text © Rob Ritchie 1998

Editorial, design and production by Hart McLeod, Cambridge

British Library Cataloguing-in-Publication Data

A CIP record for this book is available from the British Library

ISBN 1 84085 094 9

Printed and bound in Great Britain

Letts Educational is the trading name of BPP (Letts Educational) Ltd

Contents

Introduction

This Revision Guide focuses on Core Material common to all exam syllabuses for Chemistry A-level.

It also contains material extra to the core that is in **most** exam syllabuses.

It does **not** include all material for all syllabuses. At present, there are several linear syllabuses together with as many modular syllabuses. Most include some element of choice and a guide covering everything in all syllabuses would be a very big book.

You will find most of the material in this guide relevant. However, you need to use this guide alongside your syllabus. This will enable you to identify those topics that you do **not** need to learn and also those topics that you **must find elsewhere**. Some guidance is included in the margin areas.

There are some cases where different syllabuses use different definitions and these are highlighted within the text.

Where possible, examples and some specimen problems have been included, especially in topics related to the Mole, Energetics, Equilibria and Rates.

Some general hints are:

1. Learn the work, especially definitions, mechanisms and all the organic chemistry.
2. Test yourself: many definitions are included in boxes in the text and you should ensure that you master these.
3. Study the examples.
4. Make your own notes.
5. If you are studying a modular course, then use the relevant parts from this text for each module.

1 Moles and equations

Atomic mass

The **carbon-12 isotope** is chosen as the international standard for the measurement of atomic mass.

- One atom of carbon-12 has a mass of **exactly** 12 atomic mass units (a.m.u.).

Relative masses

Atoms

> The **relative atomic mass**, A_r, is the weighted average mass of an atom of the element compared with one-twelfth of the mass of an atom of the carbon-12 isotope.

Examples: H: 1.0079; Cl: 35.453; Pb: 207.19

Molecules

> The **relative molecular mass**, M_r, is the weighted average mass of a molecule of a compound compared with one-twelfth of the mass of an atom of the carbon-12 isotope.

Examples: Cl_2: $M_r = 35.45 \times 2 = 70.90$; H_2O: $M_r = (1.00 \times 2) + 16.00 = 18.00$

Formulae

> The **relative formula mass** is the weighted average mass of the formula unit of a compound compared with one-twelfth of the mass of an atom of the carbon-12 isotope.

Examples: $CaBr_2$: relative formula mass $= 40.08 + (79.91 \times 2) = 199.90$

Measuring relative atomic masses

A relative atomic mass is measured using a mass spectrometer.

- An element is bombarded with electrons.
- The positive ions are accelerated using a high voltage.
- The positive ions are deflected using a magnetic field.
- Positive ions of small mass are deflected more than ions of a large mass.
- The ions are detected to produce a *mass spectrum*.

Relative masses have **no** units

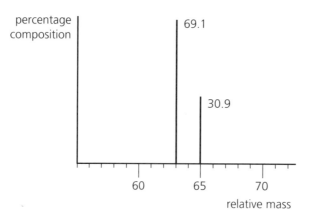

The mass spectrum of copper

ion	relative mass	% composition
$^{63}Cu^+$	63.00	69.1%
$^{65}Cu^+$	65.00	30.9%

The relative atomic mass of copper

$$= \left(\frac{69.1 \times 63.00}{100}\right) + \left(\frac{30.9 \times 65.00}{100}\right)$$

$$= \mathbf{63.62}$$

The mole

- The **mole** is the S.I. unit of *amount of substance*.
- The abbreviation for a mole is *mol*.

> 1 mole is defined as the amount of substance that contains as many particles as there are carbon atoms in exactly 12 g of the carbon-12 isotope.

- The number of atoms in 1 mole of carbon-12 is called the Avogadro constant, *L*.
- The Avogadro constant is 600,000,000,000,000,000,000,000 or 6×10^{23} mol^{-1}.

Molar mass, *M*

Moles from masses

- The molar mass is the mass of one mole of a substance, e.g. molar mass of $CO_2 = 44$ g mol^{-1}.
- The molar mass, *M*, is equal to the relative mass in grammes.

The units of molar mass are g mol^{-1}

> Amount of substance (in moles) $= \dfrac{\text{mass}}{\text{molar mass}}$ mol.

Example

Amount (in moles) of CO_2 in 11 g of $CO_2 = \dfrac{11}{44} = 0.25$ mol.

Molar gas volume

Moles from gas volumes

Avogadro's *hypothesis*:
equal volumes of gases contain the same number of molecules under the same conditions of temperature and pressure.

See also Ideal Gas Equation, pp. 12

> At room temperature and pressure (r.t.p.), 1 mole of molecules of **any** gas occupies 24.0 dm^3 (24,000 cm^3).

> At standard temperature and pressure (s.t.p.), 1 mole of molecules of **any** gas occupies 22.4 dm^3 (22,400 cm^3).

Example
How many moles of gas molecules are in 480 cm³ of a gas at r.t.p.?

$$24,000 \text{ cm}^3 \text{ contain 1 mol of gas molecules.}$$
$$1 \text{ cm}^3 \text{ contains } \frac{1}{24000} \text{ mol of gas molecules.}$$
$$\therefore 480 \text{ cm}^3 \text{ contain } \frac{1 \times 480}{24000} = 0.0200 \text{ mol of gas molecules.}$$

Molar solutions

Moles from solutions

The concentration of a solution is the number of moles of solute in 1 dm³ (1000 cm³) of solution.

An aqueous solution of NaCl of concentration **2 mol dm⁻³** contains **2 moles of NaCl** in **1 dm³** of solution.

A 2M solution has a concentration of 2 mol dm⁻³

$$\text{In general, for } V \text{ cm}^3 \text{ of a solution of concentration } c \text{ mol dm}^{-3},$$
$$\text{Number of moles} = \frac{c \times V}{1000}$$

Example: 25.0 cm³ of 2.00 mol dm⁻³ NaCl contains $\frac{2.00 \times 25.0}{1000} = 0.0500$ mol of NaCl.

Formulae and equations

Types of chemical formula

The **empirical formula** is the simplest, whole-number ratio of atoms of each element in a compound.
Example: ethane has 1 carbon atom for each 3 hydrogen atoms. The empirical formula of ethane is CH_3.

The **molecular formula** is the actual number of atoms of each element in a molecule of a compound.
Example: each molecule of ethane contains 2 carbon atoms and 6 hydrogen atoms. The molecular formula of ethane is C_2H_6.

Determination of a formula

See also Organic Chemistry pp. 84

A formula can be calculated from experimental results using the mole concept.

Example 1
What is the empirical formula of a compound formed when 6.75 g of aluminium reacts with 26.63 g of chlorine? [A_r: Al, 27.0; Cl, 35.5.]

Find the molar ratio of atoms:	Al	:	Cl
	$= \dfrac{6.75}{27.0}$	:	$\dfrac{26.63}{35.5}$
	0.25	:	0.75
Divide by smallest number (0.25):	1	:	3
$\therefore$ Empirical formula = $AlCl_3$			

Analysis often doesn't calculate the oxygen content directly but it can easily be calculated:

Example 2

What is the molecular formula of a compound containing carbon, hydrogen and oxygen only with the composition by mass of carbon: 40.0%; hydrogen: 6.7%?

[M_r = 180. A_r: H, 1.00; C, 12.0; O, 16.0.]

Percentage of oxygen in compound = 100 − (40.0 + 6.7) = 53.3%

100.0 g of the compound contains 40.0 g C, 6.7 g H and 53.3 g O.

Find the molar ratio of atoms:	C	:	H	:	O
=	$\dfrac{40.0}{12}$	:	$\dfrac{6.7}{1}$	:	$\dfrac{53.3}{16}$
	= 3.33	:	6.7	:	3.33
Divide by smallest number (3.33):	1	:	2	:	1

∴ Empirical formula = CH_2O

Relate to molecular mass:

Each CH_2O unit has a relative mass of 12 + (1 × 2) + 16 = 30

The M_r, of the compound, 180, contains 180/30 = 6 CH_2O units

∴ Molecular formula is $C_6H_{12}O_6$

Equations

Chemical reactions involve the *rearrangement* of atoms and ions.

Chemical equations provide two types of information:
- qualitative – *which* atoms or ions are rearranging
- quantitative – *how many* atoms or ions are rearranging.

Qualitative information

The formula of each substance provides information about the chemicals that are reacting together:

Examples: $2H_2(g) + O_2(g) \longrightarrow 2H_2O(l)$

hydrogen + oxygen $\longrightarrow$ water

State symbols - physical states of each species under the reaction conditions: gaseous state, (g);   liquid state, (l);   solid state, (s);   aqueous solution, (aq).

- *Balancing* of the equation accounts for all of the species in the reaction.
- In a correctly balanced equation, there will be the **same number** of atoms of each element on each side of the equation.

Quantitative information

The balancing number is the **amount** of each substance in moles:

$2H_2(g) + O_2(g) \longrightarrow 2H_2O(l)$
2 mol   1 mol $\longrightarrow$ 2 mol
2(2x1) g   (16x2) g $\longrightarrow$ 2(1x2 + 16) g
4 g   32 g $\longrightarrow$ 36 g

∴ 4 g of H_2 (g) react with 32 g O_2(g) to form 36 g of $H_2O(l)$

Example

What quantities of nitrogen and oxygen are required to form 3 g of nitrogen oxide, NO? [A_r: N, 14; O, 16.]

equation	$N_2(g)$	+	$O_2(g)$	$\longrightarrow$		$2NO(g)$
moles	**1** mol	+	**1** mol	$\longrightarrow$		**2** mol
reacting masses	(14x2)g	+	(16x2)g	$\longrightarrow$		**2**(14+16)g
	28 g	+	32 g	$\longrightarrow$		60 g
for 3 g NO(g), ÷ 20:	1.4 g	+	1.6 g	$\longrightarrow$		3 g

∴ 1.4 g of $N_2(g)$ react with 1.6 g of $O_2(g)$ to form 3 g NO(g).

Example

What volume of oxygen, at r.t.p., is formed by the decomposition of an aqueous solution containing 17 g of hydrogen peroxide, H_2O_2? [A_r: H, 1; O, 16.]

equation	$2H_2O_2(aq)$	$\longrightarrow$	$2H_2O(l)$	+	$O_2(g)$
moles	**2** mol	$\longrightarrow$	**2** mol	+	**1** mol
reacting masses	**2**{(1x2) + (16x2)}g	$\longrightarrow$	**2**{(1x2)+(16x1)}g	+	**1**x24 dm³
	68 g	$\longrightarrow$	36 g	+	24 dm³
for 17 g H_2O_2, ÷ 4:	17 g	$\longrightarrow$	9 g	+	6 dm³

∴ 17 g (0.5 mol) of H_2O_2 decomposes to form 6 dm³ of $O_2(g)$

Titrations

Acid-alkali titrations

- The acid is added from the burette to the alkali.
- An indicator is required to show the 'end-point' when all acid has reacted.

Most A-level syllabuses include these two types of titration

Redox titrations

Permanganate/reducing agent titrations

- $KMnO_4$ and a reducing agent such as Fe^{2+}.
- Purple $KMnO_4$ (aq) is added from the burette to acidified reducing agent.
- At the end-point, the colour changes from colourless to pale pink showing that all the reducing agent has reacted.

Owing to the intense purple permanganate, these titrations are self-indicating

Thiosulphate/iodine titrations

- Iodine is often liberated in a first reaction.
- $Na_2S_2O_3$ (aq) is added from the burette to the deep brown iodine solution.
- As the end-point is approached, the brown iodine colour lightens. When the iodine is a pale-straw colour, starch is added, forming a blue colouration. This improves the detection of the end-point. A dark blue precipitate forms if iodine is added too soon.
- At the end-point, the colour changes from pale blue to colourless showing that all iodine has reacted.

Starch is added to make the end-point easier to see

Titration calculations

Each titration problem relies on five pieces of information, one of which is unknown:
- a balanced equation
- the concentration c_1 of the first reagent
- the reacting volume V_1 of the first reagent
- the concentration c_2 of the second reagent
- the reacting volume V_2 of the second reagent.

Example

A titration of aqueous sodium hydroxide, NaOH(aq), with sulphuric acid, $H_2SO_4(aq)$, uses the following information:

- A balanced equation.
- The concentration c_1 and reacting volume V_1 of NaOH(aq).
- The concentration c_2 and reacting volume V_2 of $H_2SO_4(aq)$.

$$2NaOH(aq) \quad + \quad H_2SO_4(aq) \longrightarrow Na_2SO_4(aq) + 2H_2O(l)$$

c_1	V_1

c_2	V_2

Example 1

In a titration, 25.0 cm³ of 0.100 mol dm⁻³ sodium hydroxide were found to react exactly with 11.2 cm³ of sulphuric acid. Find the concentration of the sulphuric acid.

From the titration results, the number of moles of NaOH can be calculated :

$$\text{Number of moles of NaOH} = \frac{c \times V}{1000} = \frac{0.100 \times 25.0}{1000} = 0.00250 \text{ mol NaOH.}$$

From the equation, the number of moles of H_2SO_4 can be determined:

$$2NaOH(aq) \quad + \quad H_2SO_4(aq) \longrightarrow Na_2SO_4(aq) + 2H_2O(l)$$

2 mol   **1** mol *(balancing numbers)*

∴ 0.00250 mol NaOH reacts with 0.00125 mol H_2SO_4.

Number of moles of H_2SO_4 that reacted = 0.00125 mol.

The concentration in mol dm⁻³ of H_2SO_4 can now be calculated by scaling to 1000 cm³:

11.2 cm³ of H_2SO_4 (aq) contains 0.00125 mol H_2SO_4.

1 cm³ of H_2SO_4 (aq) contains $\dfrac{0.00125}{11.2} = 0.000112$ mol H_2SO_4.

1 dm³ (1000 cm³) of H_2SO_4 (aq) contains $\dfrac{0.00125}{11.2} \times 1000 = 0.112$ mol H_2SO_4.

∴ Concentration of H_2SO_4 (aq) is 0.112 mol dm⁻³.

Example 2

Five iron tablets with a combined mass of 0.900 g were dissolved in acid and made up to 100 cm³ of solution. In a titration 10.0 cm³ of this solution were found to react exactly with 10.4 cm³ of acidified 0.0100 mol dm⁻³ potassium manganate(VII). What is the percentage of iron in the tablets?

From the titration results, the number of moles of $KMnO_4$ can be calculated :

$$\text{Number of moles of } KMnO_4 = \frac{c \times V}{1000} = \frac{0.0100 \times 10.4}{1000} = 1.04 \times 10^{-4} \text{ mol } KMnO_4.$$

From the equation, the number of moles of Fe^{2+} can be determined:

$$5Fe^{2+}(aq) + MnO_4^-(aq) + 8H^+(aq) \rightarrow 5Fe^{3+}(aq) + Mn^{2+}(aq) + 4H_2O(l)$$

5 mol   **1** mol *(balancing numbers)*

∴ **5** × 1.04 × 10⁻⁴ mol Fe^{2+} react with 1.04 × 10⁻⁴ mol MnO_4^-.

∴ Number of moles of Fe^{2+} that reacted = 5.20 × 10⁻⁴ mol.

The concentration and volume of NaOH are known

Using the equation, determine the number of moles of the second reagent

Work out the concentration of $H_2SO_4(aq)$ in mol dm⁻³

The titration results are calculated as in Example 1

Find the number of moles of Fe^{2+} in the original solution prepared from the tablets:

> 10.0 cm³ of Fe^{2+}(aq) contains 5.20×10^{-4} mol Fe^{2+}
> 100 cm³ solution of iron tablets contains $10 \times (5.20 \times 10^{-4}) = 5.20 \times 10^{-3}$ mol Fe^{2+}.

Find the percentage of Fe^{2+} in the tablets (A_r: Fe, 55.8):

> 5.20×10^{-3} mol Fe^{2+} has a mass of $5.20 \times 10^{-3} \times 55.8 = 0.290$ g
> $\therefore$ % of Fe^{2+} in tablets $= \dfrac{\text{mass of } Fe^{2+}}{\text{mass of tablets}} \times 100 = \dfrac{0.290}{0.900} \times 100 = 32.2$ %

The kinetic theory of gases

Ideal gases

Assumptions of an ideal gas

- Molecules are in continuous random motion.
- Collisions are elastic.
- Molecules have mass but no volume.
- No attraction between molecules.
- Average kinetic energy of molecules is proportional to the absolute temperature.

Gas Laws

An ideal gas obeys the Gas Laws.

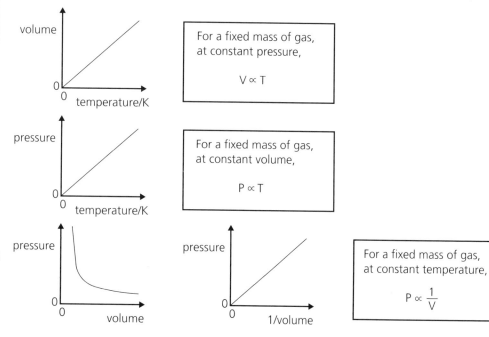

For a fixed mass of gas, at constant pressure,

$$V \propto T$$

For a fixed mass of gas, at constant volume,

$$P \propto T$$

For a fixed mass of gas, at constant temperature,

$$P \propto \frac{1}{V}$$

Real gases

A real gas departs from ideal behaviour at:
- high pressure and low temperature.

Under these conditions:
- the size of molecules becomes significant compared with the total volume occupied by the gas
- the molecules are closer together so that intermolecular forces become significant.

Polar molecules, e.g. NH_3, deviate more from ideal behaviour than non-polar molecules. They experience greater intermolecular forces.

Small, non-polar molecules, e.g. He, most closely follow ideal behaviour.

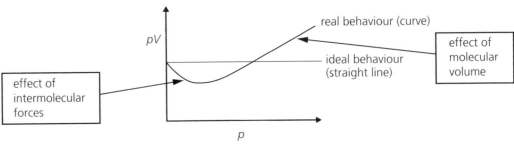

The ideal gas equation

$pV=nRT$

R is the ideal gas constant $= 8.31$ J K^{-1} mol^{-1}.

Useful gas volumes
At room temperature and pressure (r.t.p.), 298K and 100 kPa:
* 1 mole of a gas occupies 24 dm^3.
At standard temperature and pressure (s.t.p.), 273K and 100 kPa:
* 1 mole of a gas occupies 22.4 dm^3.

Units and the ideal gas equation
Pressure, p, is in Pa.
Volume, V, is in m^3.
Temperature, T, is in K.

Conversion rules

cm^3 to m^3	$\times 10^{-6}$	e.g. 10 cm^3 $= 10 \times 10^{-6}$ $= 1 \times 10^{-5}$ m^3
dm^3 to m^3	$\times 10^{-3}$	e.g. 10 dm^3 $= 10 \times 10^{-3}$ $= 1 \times 10^{-2}$ m^3
°C to K	$+ 273$	e.g. 15°C $= 15 + 273$ $= 288$ K
kPa to Pa	$\times 10^3$	e.g. 200 kPa $= 200 \times 10^3$ $= 2 \times 10^5$ Pa

The determination of M_r

The usual method is to vaporise a known mass of a volatile liquid in a gas syringe.

Example
A 0.215 g sample of a volatile liquid, **X**, produces 77.5 cm^3 of gas at 100°C and 100 kPa. Calculate the relative molecular mass of **X**.

Convert values:

77.5 cm^3	$= 77.5 \times 10^{-6}$ m^3	$= 7.75 \times 10^{-5}$ m^3
100°C	$= 100 + 273$ K	$= 373$ K
100 kPa	$= 100 \times 10^3$ Pa	$= 1.00 \times 10^5$ Pa

Find the number of moles using the ideal gas equation:

$$pV = nRT \quad \therefore n = \frac{pV}{RT}$$

$$\therefore n = \frac{1.00 \times 10^5 \times 7.75 \times 10^{-5}}{8.31 \times 373} = 0.00250 \text{ mol}$$

Find M and M_r from the mass and the number of moles:

$$n = \frac{mass}{M}$$

$$\therefore M = \frac{mass}{n} = \frac{0.215}{0.00250} = 86.0 \text{ g mol}^{-1}$$

$$\therefore M_r = 86.0$$

2 Atomic structure

The chemist's atom

nucleus
(protons
+
neutrons)

electron
shells

The properties of sub-atomic particles

particle	relative mass	relative charge
proton	1	1+
neutron	1	0
electron	negligible	1–

All atoms are electrically neutral.

- The number of electrons in the shells is the same as the number of protons in the nucleus.
- The mass is made up almost entirely from the masses of the protons and neutrons.
- The mass of the proton is virtually identical to the mass of a neutron.

Isotopes

The mass number is sometimes known as the nucleon number

Elements exist naturally as a mixture of *isotopes.*

- Isotopes are atoms of the same element with different masses.
- Isotopes of an element have the same number of protons as electrons.
- Each isotope has a different number of neutrons in the nucleus.

Isotopes of carbon

The atomic number is sometimes known as the proton number

Carbon exists as three isotopes, ^{12}C, ^{13}C, ^{14}C.

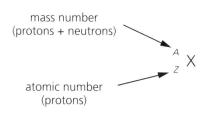

mass number
(protons + neutrons)

$^{A}_{Z}X$

atomic number
(protons)

	protons	neutrons	electrons
$^{12}_{6}C$	6	6	6
$^{13}_{6}C$	6	7	6
$^{14}_{6}C$	6	8	6

- The number of protons in the nucleus identifies an element – an atom of C always has 6 protons.
- The nucleus has nothing to do with chemical reactions – these involve the electrons.

The electronic structure of the atom

Orbitals

An orbital holds up to two electrons

Electrons exist in negative *charge clouds* called *orbitals*.

- An orbital can hold up to two electrons.
- There are four known types of orbital, *s, p, d* and *f*-orbitals.

1 type of s orbital

s-orbitals

- There is one type of *s*-orbital, spherical in shape.

3 types of p orbital

p-orbitals

- There are 3 types of *p*-orbital, at right angles to one another, p_x, p_y and p_z.
- Each *p*-orbital forms a 3–dimensional dumb-bell shape.

s-orbital

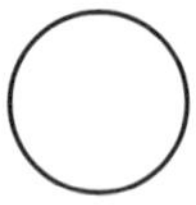

p-orbital

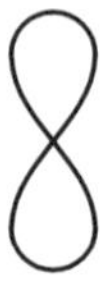

three *p*-orbitals

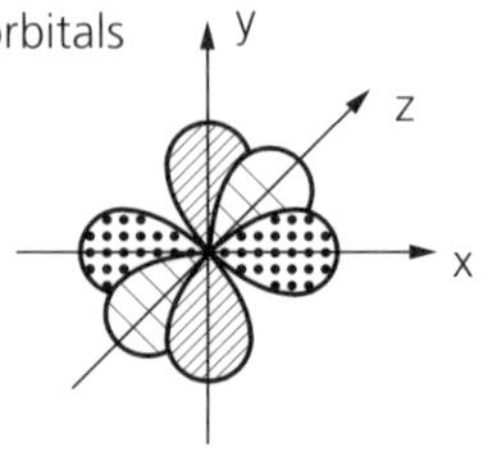

5 types of d orbital

d-orbitals and f-orbitals

The structures of *d* and *f*-orbitals are more complex.

7 types of f orbital

- There are 5 types of *d*-orbital.
- There are 7 types of *f*-orbital.

Sub-shells

A sub-shell is a collection of orbitals

- A sub-shell is a collection of orbitals.

The four types of sub-shell are shown below:

sub-shell	orbitals	maximum electrons
s	1	$1 \times 2 = 2$
p	3	$3 \times 2 = 6$
d	5	$5 \times 2 = 10$
f	7	$7 \times 2 = 14$

Principal quantum shells or 'shells'

The principal quantum shell, n, is the shell number

- A shell is a collection of sub-shells.
- Each successive shell contains an additional type of sub-shell.
- Each successive shell is at a higher energy.
- The first four principal quantum shells are shown below:

Shells are also referred to as 'energy levels'

principal quantum shell	sub-shell				maximum electrons	
1	1*s*				2	2
2	2*s*	2*p*			2 + 6	8
3	3*s*	3*p*	3*d*		2 + 6 + 10	18
4	4*s*	4*p*	4*d*	4*f*	2 + 6 + 10 + 14	32

How many electrons are found in each shell?

- Number of electrons = $2n^2$ (*n* = principal quantum shell)

Rules for placing electrons in an atom

Filling of orbitals

- An orbital can hold up to 2 electrons.
- Each electron can have one of two opposite spins.
- Within an orbital, each electron of a pair must have an opposite spin.

allowed   not allowed

Filling of sub-shells and shells

- Each energy level splits into its sub-shell energy levels.
- The electrons occupy sub-shells in order of their energy levels.

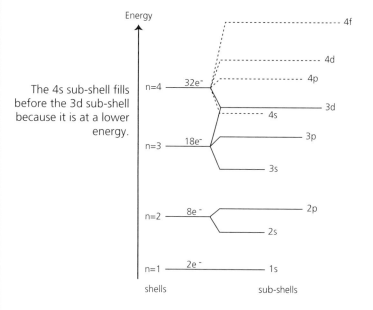

The 4s sub-shell fills before the 3d sub-shell because it is at a lower energy.

- The orbitals in a sub-shell are filled singly with parallel spins before pairing occurs.

Nitrogen, N, has 7 electrons: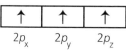

$1s$ $2s$ $2p_x$ $2p_y$ $2p_z$

- The electronic configuration of N is $1s^2 2s^2 2p_x^1 2p_y^1 2p_z^1$ or, $1s^2 2s^2 2p^3$.

Sub-shells and the Periodic Table
- The Periodic Table is structured in sub-shell blocks of 2, 6, 10 and 14.
- This makes it easy to predict the electronic configuration of any element.

	1s	

s-block				p-block
2s				2p
3s		d-block		3p
4s		3d		4p
5s		4d		5p
6s		5d		6p
7s				

f-block
4f
5f

Ionisation energy

- Ionisation energy measures the ease with which an atom loses an electron.

The first ionisation energy

> *The first ionisation energy* of an element is the energy required to remove **1 electron** from each atom in **1 mole** of **gaseous atoms** to form 1 mole of gaseous 1+ ions.

A common exam definition. Don't forget the gaseous atoms

$$Na(g) \longrightarrow Na^+(g) \quad + \quad e^-$$

1 mole of **gaseous atoms**	**1 mole** of **gaseous 1+ ions**	**1 mole** of **electrons**

Successive ionisation energies

The energy to remove each electron in turn is the *successive* ionisation energy.
For example, the fourth ionisation energy for sodium would represent the following:

$$Na^{3+}(g) \longrightarrow Na^{4+}(g) \quad + \quad e^-$$

1 mole of **gaseous 3+ ions**	**1 mole** of **gaseous 4+ ions**	**1 mole** of **electrons**

Each successive ionisation energy gets larger

As each electron is removed:

- the **same** number of protons attracts **fewer** electrons
- there is less repulsion between the electrons that remain
- the remaining electrons are pulled in closer to the nucleus, increasing the attraction
- each successive ionisation energy gets larger.

Evidence for shells from successive ionisation energies

The successive ionisation energies of sodium

A large increase in successive ionisation energy marks the removal of an electron from a different shell, at a lower energy level

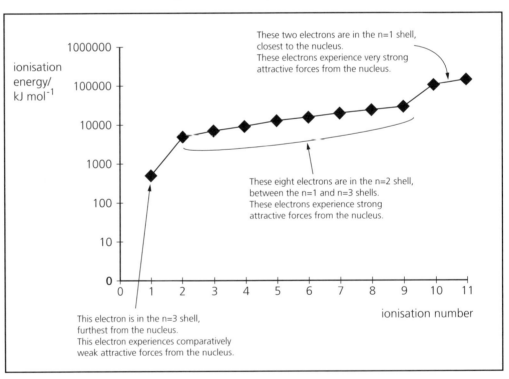

This pattern shows that a sodium atom has three shells:

- the first shell, n=1, contains two electrons
- the second shell, n=2, contains eight electrons
- the third shell, n=3, contains one electron.

Factors affecting ionisation energy

Three factors affect the attraction of the positive nucleus for negative electrons

Distance
- Increasing the distance between nucleus and electrons reduces the attractive force.
- ∴ ionisation energy **decreases**.

Nuclear charge
- Increasing the number of protons in the nucleus increases the attractive force.
- ∴ ionisation energy **increases**.

Electronic shielding or 'screening'
The outer shell electrons are 'shielded' or 'screened' from the nuclear charge by the repulsion of the inner electrons.
- ∴ the overall attractive force experienced by the outer electrons decreases.
- ∴ ionisation energy **decreases**.

Ionisation energy and the Periodic Table

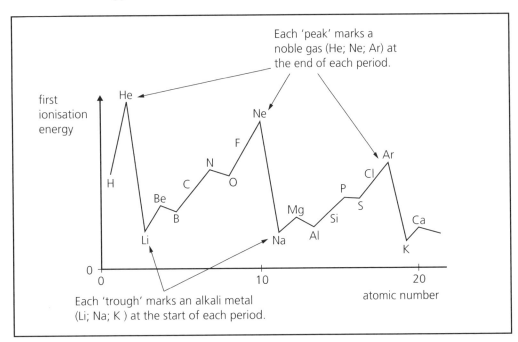

Trends across a period
- Nuclear charge increases.
- Electrons are added to the **same shell** that is the **same order of distance** from the nucleus.
- Same degree of shielding.
- Outer electrons experience greater attraction.
- The first ionisation energy increases across a period.

Across a period, increasing nuclear charge is most important

Trends down a group
- Nuclear charge increases.
- Electrons are added to the **new shell**, further from the nucleus.
- Number of inner shells is greater leading to increased shielding of outer electrons.
- Outer electrons experience less attraction.
- The first ionisation energy decreases down a group.

Down a group, increasing distance and shielding are most important

Evidence for sub-shells from ionisation energies

Variation in the first ionisation energies across Period 2

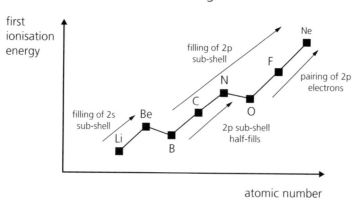

Comparing beryllium and boron
Boron has a lower first ionisation energy than beryllium.

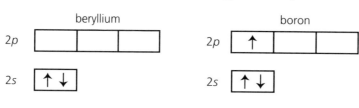

- 2s sub-shell full

- 2p sub-shell starts to fill
- higher energy level
- electron easier to remove
- drop in first I.E.

Comparing nitrogen and oxygen
Oxygen has a lower first ionisation energy than nitrogen.

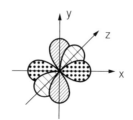

- 2p sub-shell half-full
- 1 electron in each 2p orbital

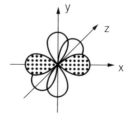

- 2p electrons start to pair
- paired electrons repel
- electron easier to remove
- drop in first I.E.

> Stable electron structures are often associated with:
> full shells, full sub-shells, half-full sub-shells

3 Bonding and structure

Chemical bonding

Stable atoms
The noble gases exist as single atoms that are very unreactive.
In the atoms of a noble gas:
- all electrons are paired
- the bonding shells are full.

He atom Ne atom Ar atom

Bonding

Atoms join together with forces called chemical bonds.
When bonds form, unpaired electrons *often* pair up to form a noble gas electron structure.
This is often referred to as the 'octet rule':
- the bonding shells are full
- the electron structure is very stable.

The 'octet rule' is useful, but it is not always the case. A better general 'rule' is:
- when bonds form, unpaired *s* and *p* electrons pair up.

unreactive Ne atom with   reactive F atom with
all electrons paired   an unpaired electron

Ne atom   F atom
2,8   2,7

Unpaired electrons are rarely encountered in natural chemicals.

Types of bonding

Chemical bonds are classified into two main types: ionic and covalent.
- **Ionic** bonding occurs between a **metal** and a **non-metal**.
- **Covalent** bonding occurs between a **non-metal** and a **non-metal**.

Always decide the type of bonding before:
- drawing a 'dot-and-cross' diagram
- predicting how a compound reacts
- predicting the properties of a compound.

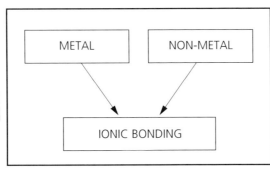   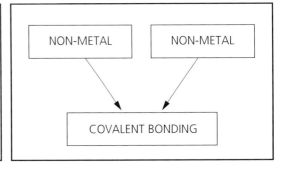

Many mistakes are made in chemistry by confusing the type of bonding.

Covalent and ionic compounds are bonded differently and they behave differently.

You cannot apply 'ionic bonding ideas' to a compound that is covalent

Ionic bonds

Ionic bonds are present in a compound of a metal and a non-metal

- Electrons are **transferred** from a metal atom to a non-metal atom forming **ions**.
- An ionic bond is the *electrical attraction* between the oppositely charged ions.

Example 1
Sodium chloride, NaCl

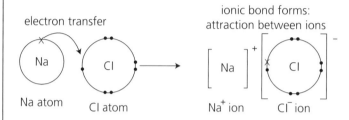

The ions that are formed often have stable noble gas electron structures with full outer electron shells.

In these 'dot-and-cross' diagrams, only the outer shell electrons involved in the formation of ionic bonds are shown

Example 2
Magnesium chloride, $MgCl_2$
Two Cl atoms are needed for the outer shell electrons of a Mg atom.

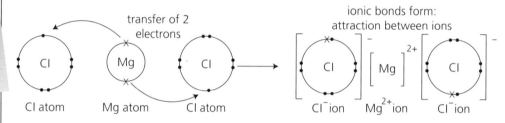

Ionic charges and the Periodic Table

Some elements can form ions with different charges:
iron(II): Fe^{2+}
iron(III): Fe^{3+}.
See also Transition elements and Redox

Group	1	2	3	4	5	6	7	8
number of outer shell electrons	1	2	3	4	5	6	7	8
element	Li	Be	B	C	N	O	F	Ne
	2,1	2,2	2,3	2,4	2,5	2,6	2,7	2,8
ion	Li^+	Be^{2+}			N^{3-}	O^{2-}	F^-	
	2	2			2,8	2,8	2,8	
element	Na	Mg	Al	Si	P	S	Cl	Ar
	2,8,1	2,8,2	2,8,3	2,8,4	2,8,5	2,8,6	2,8,7	2,8,8
ion	Na^+	Mg^{2+}	Al^{3+}		P^{3-}	S^{2-}	Cl^-	
	2,8	2,8	2,8		2,8,8	2,8,8	2,8,8	

Molecular ions

Learn these

1+		1−		2−		3−	
ammonium	NH_4^+	hydroxide	OH^-	carbonate	CO_3^{2-}	phosphate	PO_4^{3-}
		nitrate	NO_3^-	sulphate	SO_4^{2-}		
		nitrite	NO_2^-	sulphite	SO_3^{2-}		

Predicting ionic formulae

calcium chloride:	ion	charge
	Ca^{2+}	2+
equalise charges		
	Cl^-	1−
	Cl^-	1−
total charge should be zero:		0
formula		$CaCl_2$

aluminium sulphate:	ion	charge
	Al^{3+}	3+
	Al^{3+}	3+
equalise charges		
	SO_4^{2-}	2−
	SO_4^{2-}	2−
	SO_4^{2-}	2−
total charge should be zero:		0
formula		$Al_2(SO_4)_3$

Covalent bonds

> A covalent bond is a *shared pair* of electrons.

A covalent bond is formed:
- between atoms of non-metals with a similar attraction for electrons
- when two atoms attract the same pair of electrons resulting in overlap of orbitals.

Covalent bonds are present in a compound of two non-metals

Unless otherwise instructed, show outer shells only for bonding diagrams

Single covalent bonds

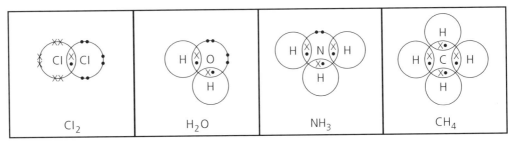

Cl_2 H_2O NH_3 CH_4

Multiple covalent bonds

Double and triple bonds are possible:

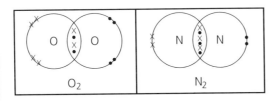

O_2 N_2

Dative covalent bonds

- A dative covalent bond forms when the *shared pair* of electrons originates from just one of the atoms.

Example
The formation of the ammonium ion, NH_4^+

The involvement of the electron pair as a dative covalent bond is often shown as:

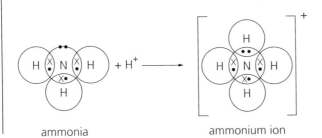

ammonia   ammonium ion

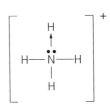

Shapes of molecules

- The pairs of electrons that surround an atom repel one another.
  ∴ The electron pairs become as far apart as possible:

In exams, these are easy marks provided that the facts have been learnt

Learn these shapes and bond angles

molecule	$BeCl_2$	BF_3	CH_4	SF_6
electron pairs around central atom	2	3	4	6
dot-and-cross diagram				
shape	linear	trigonal planar	tetrahedral	octahedral
bond angle	Cl—Be—Cl 180°	F—B—F 120°	H—C—H 109.5°	F—S—F 90°

Molecules with lone pairs

A lone pair is closer to an atom than a bonded pair of electrons.
The relative magnitudes of electron-pair repulsions are:

- **lone**-pair/**lone**-pair > **bonded**-pair/**lone**-pair > **bonded**-pair/**bonded**-pair repulsion.

Lone pairs distort the shape of a molecule and reduce the bond angle:

Always draw 3–D shapes – you may be penalised in exams otherwise

molecule	CH_4	NH_3	H_2O
number of lone pairs	0	1	2
dot-and-cross diagram			
shape	tetrahedral	pyramidal	non-linear
bond angle	109.5°	107°	104.5°

Double bonds

- Each double bond is treated in the same way as a bonded pair.
- Each double bond and pair of electrons should be treated as a 'bonding region'.

molecule	number of bonding regions	'dot-and-cross' diagram	shape	bond angle
CO_2	2		linear	O=C=O 180°

Polar and non-polar molecules

Electronegativity

- The nuclei of the atoms in a molecule attract the pair of electrons in a covalent bond.
- Electronegativity is the relative attraction of a bonded atom for the pair of electrons in a bond.
- Electronegativity depends upon the element.

Non-polar bonds

- The bonded atoms are the same and have the same electronegativity.
- The bonded electrons in a **non-polar** covalent bond are shared **equally** between both atoms.

Example H_2 and Cl_2

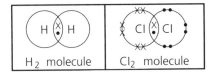

H_2 molecule	Cl_2 molecule

Polar bonds

- The bonded atoms are different and each has a different electronegativity.
- The bonded electrons in a covalent bond are pulled towards the more electronegative of the atoms.
- The electrons in the bond are shared **unequally** making a *polar bond*.

Example HCl: Cl is more electronegative than H

$\delta+$ $\delta-$

$H \overset{x}{\underset{\bullet}{\text{———}}} Cl$

electron pair pulled
closer to chlorine

- The HCl molecule is '**polarised**'
- −a *polar* molecule with a *permanent dipole*.

Symmetrical and unsymmetrical molecules

If the molecule is symmetrical, the dipoles will cancel and the molecule will not have a permanent dipole.

Example Molecules of $CHCl_3$ and CCl_4

electron pairs pulled closer to chlorine	no overall dipole electron pairs pulled equally
$CHCl_3$ - polar	CCl_4 - non-polar

Intermolecular forces

- **Van der Waals' forces** exist between all molecules whether polar or non-polar.
- Without these forces, non-polar molecules could never form a liquid or a solid.
Example Van der Waals' forces in liquid neon.

- electrons cause an oscillating dipole

dipole continually changes with time

dipole oscillates

δδ+   δδ−   δδ−   δδ+

induced dipole ripples between molecules

- oscillating dipole induces a dipole in a neighbouring molecule which is induced onto further molecules

δδ−   δδ+   δδ−   δδ+   δδ−   δδ+   δδ−   δδ+   δδ−   δδ+

instantaneous dipoles attract each other

- Molecules with more electrons will generate larger oscillating and induced dipoles.
- These produce larger attractive forces between molecules.

Van der Waals' forces and electrons

group 8	b. pt./°C	number of electrons	trend
He	−269	2	
Ne	−246	10	• easier to distort electron cloud
Ar	−186	18	• induced dipoles increase
Kr	−152	36	• intermolecular forces increase
Xe	−107	54	
Rn	−62	88	• boiling point increases

Dipole-dipole interactions

- A polar molecule will attract another polar molecule by the small δ+ and δ− charges.
- This gives a weak *intermolecular force* called a permanent-dipole/permanent-dipole interaction.

Example Intermolecular forces between HCl molecules

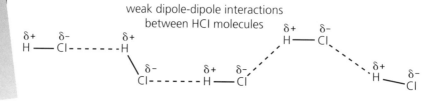

weak dipole-dipole interactions between HCl molecules

Hydrogen bonds

A hydrogen bond (H-bond) is a strong intermolecular attraction between:

- a polar hydrogen atom on one molecule and
- a lone pair of electrons on a highly electronegative atom of F, O or N on a different molecule.

H-bonding is found between molecules containing the following groups:

$$\overset{\delta+}{H} \longrightarrow \overset{\delta-}{\overset{\cdots}{O}} \qquad \overset{\delta+}{H} \longrightarrow \overset{\delta-}{\overset{\cdots}{N}} \qquad \overset{\delta+}{H} \longrightarrow \overset{\delta-}{\overset{\cdots}{F}}$$

Example Hydrogen bonding between water molecules

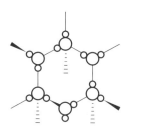

hydrogen bond formed by attraction between dipoles

Note the role of the lone pair – this is essential in hydrogen bonding

Special properties of water arising from hydrogen bonding

Solid is less dense than liquid
- Particles in solids are usually packed slightly closer together than in liquids – solids are usually more dense than liquids.
- Relatively strong hydrogen bonds hold water molecules apart in an open lattice structure.
- ∴ Ice is less dense than water.

The open hydrogen-bonded lattice of ice:

hydrogen bonds break

MELTING OF ICE

lattice collapses: molecules move closer together

Relatively high melting point and boiling point
- Relatively strong attraction (H-bonds) between H_2O molecules.
- The H-bonds are extra forces, over and above van der Waals' forces.
- These extra forces result in higher melting and boiling points than would be expected from just van der Waals' forces.
- When the ice lattice breaks, hydrogen bonds are broken.
- The covalent bonds between the H and O atoms in a H_2O molecule are strong and do not break.

Other properties
The extra intermolecular bonding from hydrogen bonds also explains the relatively high surface tension and viscosity in water.

Hydrogen bonding in other molecules

- Especially important in organic chemistry where compounds with –OH or –NH can hydrogen bond, e.g. alcohols, carboxylic acids, amines, amino acids.
- H-bonding increases when more than one –OH group is present, e.g. glycerol: $CH_2OHCHOHCH_2OH$.

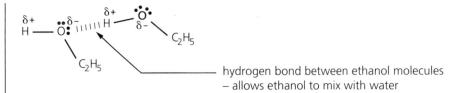

hydrogen bond between ethanol molecules
– allows ethanol to mix with water

Make sure that you can draw H-bonds between any examples, e.g. between ethanol molecules

Metallic bonding

A metallic bond is the attraction between metal ions and free electrons.

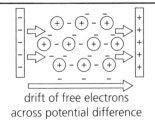

the 'sea of electrons'

The lattice is held together by electrical attraction between the + ions and the – electrons.

Electrons are mobile and are free to move throughout the lattice.

In forming the metallic lattice, each metal atom forms + ions by releasing its outer electrons to the 'sea of electrons'

Properties

High melting point and boiling point

- Strong attraction between ions and electrons in most metals.
- Generally high temperatures are needed to provide enough energy to pull the ions and electrons apart – most metals have a high m & b pt.

Electrical conductivity

Metals always conduct electricity.

drift of free electrons across potential difference

- The electrons are free to flow between positive ions, even when the metal is solid.
- Positive ions do not move.

A metallic lattice is held together by electrostatic attraction between positive metal ions and electrons

Solubility

- Metals are insoluble. Solvents such as water are unable to form strong enough forces with the ions and electrons to pull the lattice apart.

The strength of bonds

Ionic and covalent bonds

Ionic and covalent bonds are of comparable strength.

Comparing the strength of covalent bonds with intermolecular forces

type of bond	bond energy /kJ mol^{-1}
covalent bond	200–500
hydrogen bond	5–40
van der Waals' forces	~2

It is a common misconception that an ionic bond is strong whereas a covalent bond is weak. This is WRONG

How properties are related to bonding and structure

Properties of ionic compounds e.g. NaCl

High melting point and boiling point

- The attraction is strong between + and − ions.
- Each ion is surrounded by oppositely-charged ions, forming a giant ionic lattice:

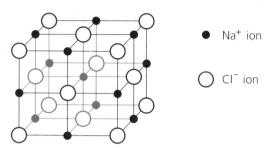

- Na$^+$ ion
- ○ Cl$^-$ ion

Solids at room temperature – high melting and boiling points - strong forces between ions

- each Na$^+$ ion surrounds 6 Cl$^-$ ions $\left.\right\}$ 6:6 coordination
- each Cl$^-$ ion surrounds 6 Na$^+$ ions
- High temperatures are needed to provide enough energy to pull the ions apart – high m & b pt.

Electrical conductivity

In the **solid** lattice,
- the ions are in a fixed position
- there are no mobile charge carriers
- ∴ non-conductor of electricity.

Conduct only when ions move free from the lattice – when molten or an aqueous solution

When melted or dissolved in water, the solid lattice breaks down
- the ions are now free to move
- the ions are now mobile charge carriers
- ∴ conductor of electricity.

Solubility

- The ionic lattice dissolves in **polar** solvents (e.g. water).
- The polar water molecules break down the lattice and surround each ion in solution.
- Each ion becomes 'solvated' with water molecules.

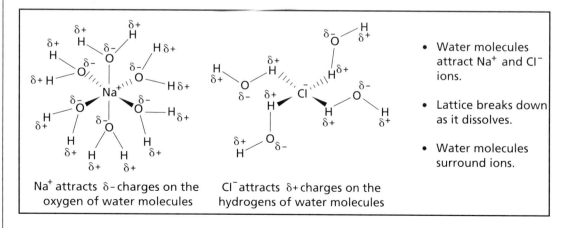

Na$^+$ attracts δ− charges on the oxygen of water molecules

Cl$^-$ attracts δ+ charges on the hydrogens of water molecules

- Water molecules attract Na$^+$ and Cl$^-$ ions.
- Lattice breaks down as it dissolves.
- Water molecules surround ions.

Properties of covalent compounds

Elements and compounds with covalent bonds exist as two types of structure.

Simple molecular structure
- Small molecules with **weak** van der Waals' forces between them, e.g. Ne, H_2, O_2, N_2.

Giant molecular structure
- Thousands of atoms bonded together with **strong** covalent bonds, e.g. diamond, graphite, SiO_2.

Properties of a simple molecular structure, e.g. I_2

Low melting point and boiling point
- Weak attraction between I_2 molecules (van der Waals' forces).
- Low temperatures are enough to provide the energy to pull the I_2 molecules apart.

Simple molecular lattice of solid I_2

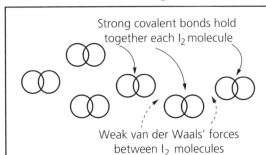

Strong covalent bonds hold together each I_2 molecule

Weak van der Waals' forces between I_2 molecules

- When the I_2 lattice breaks, only the weak van der Waals' forces between the I_2 molecules break.
- The covalent bond **between** the I atoms in the I_2 molecule is strong and it does not break when the lattice breaks down.

Electrical conductivity
- There are no free charged particles.
- ∴ Non-conductors of electricity.

Solubility
- The lattice dissolves in **non-polar** solvents (e.g. hexane).
- Hexane molecules form van der Waals' forces with I_2 molecules, breaking down the lattice.

Properties of a giant molecular structure

High melting point and boiling point
- Strong attraction between atoms (covalent forces).
- High temperatures are needed to break the strong covalent bonds in the lattice.

Solubility
- Strong covalent bonds are too strong to be broken by solvents, polar **or** non-polar.
- ∴ Giant molecular structures are insoluble in either polar or non-polar solvents.

Electrical conductivity
- There are no free charged particles (except graphite).
- ∴ Non-conductors of electricity (except graphite).

Comparison between the properties of diamond and graphite

	diamond		graphite	
structure	*tetrahedral*	*symmetrical structure held together by strong covalent bonds throughout lattice*	*hexagonal layers*	*strong layer structure but with weak bonds between the layers*
electrical conductivity	*poor* ● there are no free electrons as all outer electrons used up in the covalent bonds		*good* ● delocalised electrons between layers. ● electrons are free to move parallel to the layers when a voltage is applied.	
hardness	*hard* ● tetrahedral shape enables forces to be shared throughout the lattice		*soft* ● bonding within each layer is strong but ● weak forces between layers break easily allowing layers to slide	

A high melting point is the result of any giant structure, bonded together with strong forces. Giant structures can be ionic, covalent or metallic

Summary of properties from structure and bonding

structure	melting pt / boiling pt	reason	electrical conductivity	reason	solubility	reason
giant ionic	high	strong electrostatic attraction between ions	poor when solid good when aqueous or molten	ions in a fixed position in lattice lattice has broken down: mobile ions	good in polar solvents, e.g. water	attraction between ionic lattice and polar solvent
simple molecular	low	weak van der Waals' forces between molecules	poor	no mobile charged particles (electrons or ions)	good in non-polar solvents	van der Waals' forces between molecule and solvent
giant molecular	high	strong covalent bonds between atoms	poor	no free charged particles (electrons or ions)	poor	forces within lattice too strong for solvents to break
hydrogen bonded	low *but* higher than expected	dipole-dipole attraction between molecules	poor	no free charged particles (electrons or ions)	good in polar solvents, e.g. water	attraction between dipoles
giant metallic	usually high	strong electrostatic attraction between ions and electrons	good	free electrons, even in solid state	poor	forces within lattice too strong for solvents to break

4 The Periodic Table

The Periodic Table

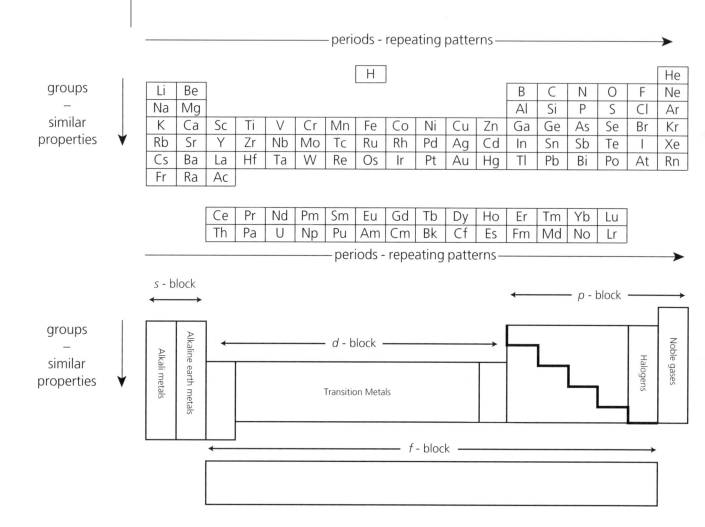

Periods and groups

In the Periodic Table, elements are arranged in order of increasing atomic number.
- Periods are horizontal rows across which there is a trend in properties.
- Groups are vertical columns including elements with similar properties.
- The 4 blocks (*s*, *p*, *d* & *f*) show the sub-shell being filled.

Metals and non-metals

- The diagonal stepped-line separates metals (to the left) from non-metals (to the right).
- Elements close to the line are 'semi-metals' and they may show properties intermediate between those of a metal and a non-metal, e.g. Si, Ge.

Periodicity

- A periodic trend or 'periodicity' in properties is repeated across each period,
  e.g.   Period 2   METAL $\longrightarrow$ NON-METAL
         Period 3   METAL $\longrightarrow$ NON-METAL
- This periodicity (repeating trend) of properties means that predictions can be made about the likely properties of an element and its compounds.
- BUT, consideration is also required of any trend in properties down a group.

Periodic trends in physical properties

Trends in atomic radii

Across a period

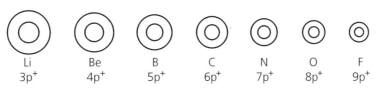

| Li | Be | B | C | N | O | F |
| $3p^+$ | $4p^+$ | $5p^+$ | $6p^+$ | $7p^+$ | $8p^+$ | $9p^+$ |

number of protons increases

radius decreases

Across the period from Li $\longrightarrow$ F:
- the nuclear charge increases
- electrons are being added to the same shell
- extra attractive force between the nucleus and electrons
- $\therefore$ the atomic radius decreases across a period.

Down a group

Down any group:
- extra shells are added that are further from the nucleus
- there are more shells between the outer electrons and the nucleus leading to greater shielding
- less attractive force on the electrons in the outer shell
- $\therefore$ the atomic radius increases down a group.

shells increase

shielding increases

atomic radius increases

> The atomic radius:
> - decreases across a period
> - increases down a group.

The same ideas are used to discuss ionisation energies pp. 16–18

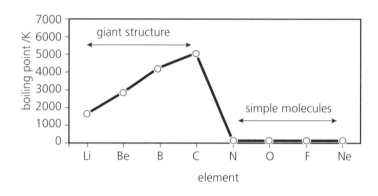

Trends in boiling point

Across a period, there is a rise to group 4 with a sharp fall between group 4 and group 5

- The fall marks a change from giant to simple molecular structures.

Period 2

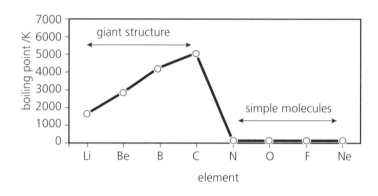

Period 3

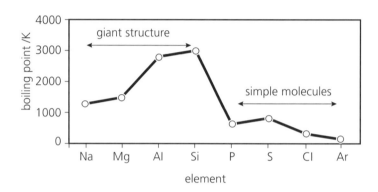

The structure of elements in Periods 2 and 3

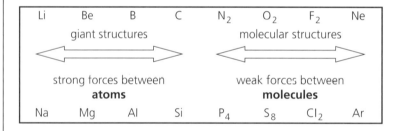

Comparison of the boiling points of the metals

- Note the increase in boiling points from groups 1 to 3 (Li →B; Na →Al).
- Related to the increasing attractive forces within the metallic lattice.
- The increase in the number of free electrons also explains an increase in electrical conductivity from Na →Al.

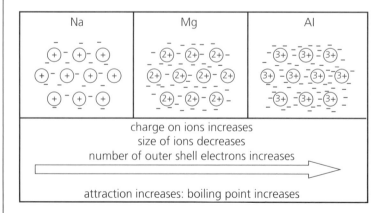

Side margin notes:

Trends in boiling point provide information about structure: giant or simple molecular

Strong forces broken: giant structure high boiling point

Weak forces broken: simple molecular structure low boiling point

Oxides and chlorides of Period 3

AlCl₃ exists as Al₂Cl₆ when solid. For simplicity, AlCl₃ is used throughout this text. Check your syllabus

Patterns in formulae

- Patterns in formula are explained by the number of electrons in the outer shell.
- The oxidation state indicates the number of electrons involved in bonding.

Chlorides

- The highest oxidation state is usually the group number.

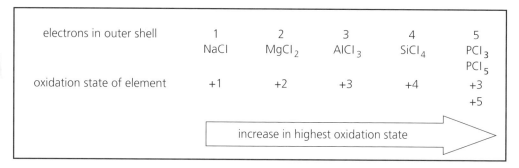

electrons in outer shell	1 $NaCl$	2 $MgCl_2$	3 $AlCl_3$	4 $SiCl_4$	5 PCl_3 PCl_5
oxidation state of element	+1	+2	+3	+4	+3 +5

increase in highest oxidation state →

See also oxidation state pp. 79–81

A periodicity (repeating trend) is seen across Periods 2, 3 and 4:

Period 2	$LiCl$	$BeCl_2$	BCl_3	CCl_4
Period 3	$NaCl$	$MgCl_2$	$AlCl_3$	$SiCl_4$
Period 4	KCl	$CaCl_2$	$GaCl_3$	$GeCl_4$

Note the trend per mole of atoms of the element in the highest chloride:

For each element in the period, there is an increase of 1 mole of Cl per mole of element

$NaCl$ $MgCl_2$ $AlCl_3$ $SiCl_4$ PCl_5

Oxides

electrons in outer shell	1 Na_2O	2 MgO	3 Al_2O_3	4 SiO_2	5 P_4O_6 P_4O_{10}	6 SO_2 SO_3
oxidation state of element	+1	+2	+3	+4	+3 +5	+4 +6

increase in highest oxidation state →

A periodicity (repeating trend) is seen across Periods 2 and 4:

Period 2	Li_2O	BeO	Be_2O_3	CO_2
Period 3	Na_2O	MgO	Al_2O_3	SiO_2
Period 4	K_2O	CaO	Ga_2O_3	GeO_2

Note the trend per mole of atoms of the element in the highest oxide:

For each element in the period, there is an increase of 0.5 mole of O per mole of element

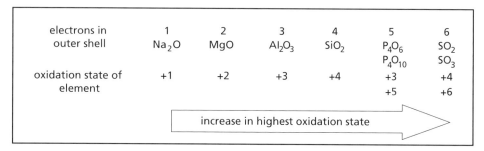

$Na_1O_{0.5}$ Mg_1O_1 $Al_1O_{1.5}$ Si_1O_2 $P_1O_{2.5}$ S_1O_3

Oxides of Period 3

Preparation

The oxides are made by reacting the element with oxygen.

Metal oxides

$$4Na(s) + O_2(g) \xrightarrow{\text{yellow flame}} 2Na_2O(s)$$

$$2Mg(s) + O_2(g) \xrightarrow{\text{white flame}} 2MgO(s)$$

$$4Al(s) + 3O_2(g) \xrightarrow{\text{white flame}} 2Al_2O_3(s)$$

Non-metal oxides

$$4P(s) + 5O_2(g) \xrightarrow{\text{white flame}} P_4O_{10}(s)$$

$$S(s) + O_2(g) \xrightarrow{\text{blue flame}} SO_2(g)$$

SO_2 reacts further with oxygen in the presence of a catalyst (V_2O_5):

$$2SO_2(g) + O_2(g) \longrightarrow 2SO_3(s)$$

The action of water on the oxides of Period 3

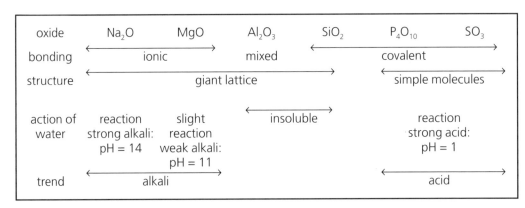

oxide	Na_2O	MgO	Al_2O_3	SiO_2	P_4O_{10}	SO_3
bonding	← ionic →		mixed	← covalent →		
structure	← giant lattice →			← simple molecules →		
action of water	reaction strong alkali: pH = 14	slight reaction weak alkali: pH = 11	← insoluble →		reaction strong acid: pH = 1	
trend	← alkali →			← acid →		

The very strong lattices in Al_2O_3 and SiO_2 cannot be broken down by water.

Reactions of metal oxides
- The metal oxides form alkalis in water:

$$Na_2O(s) + H_2O(l) \longrightarrow 2NaOH(aq) \qquad pH=14$$
$$MgO(s) + H_2O(l) \longrightarrow Mg(OH)_2(aq) \qquad pH=11$$

(MgO is slightly soluble in water and only forms a weak alkali.)

Reactions of non-metal oxides
- The non-metal oxides form acids in water:

$$P_4O_{10}(s) + 6H_2O(l) \longrightarrow 4H_3PO_4(aq) \quad phosphoric\ acid$$
$$SO_2(g) + H_2O(l) \longrightarrow H_2SO_3(aq) \quad sulphurous\ acid$$
$$SO_3(s) + H_2O(l) \longrightarrow H_2SO_4(aq) \quad sulphuric\ acid$$

Na₂O, MgO are white ionic compounds

Al₂O₃ is a white compound with bonding intermediate between ionic and covalent

P₄O₁₀ and SO₂ are covalent compounds.
P₄O₁₀: white solid
SO₂: colourless gas

Metal oxides are basic oxides, non-metal oxides are acidic oxides

Alkalis are soluble hydroxides. Alkalis contain OH⁻ ions

Acids contain H⁺ ions

Phosphor and sulph exist as P₄ S₈ molecul. These ar usually simplified equations a and S

Chlorides of Period 3

Preparation

The chlorides are made by reacting the element with chlorine.

Metal chlorides

$$2Na(s) + Cl_2(g) \longrightarrow 2NaCl(s)$$
$$Mg(s) + Cl_2(g) \longrightarrow MgCl_2(s)$$
$$2Al(s) + 3Cl_2(g) \longrightarrow 2AlCl_3(s)$$

Non-metal chlorides

$$Si(s) + 2Cl_2(g) \longrightarrow SiCl_4(l)$$
$$2P(s) + 5Cl_2(g) \longrightarrow 2PCl_5(s)$$

The action of water on the chlorides of Period 3

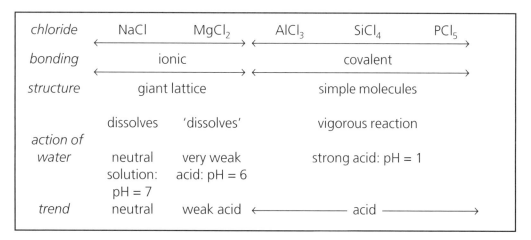

- ionic chlorides form neutral solutions in water
- covalent chlorides form acids in water

Why do chlorides act differently with water?

Dissolving of metal chlorides

The ionic chlorides dissolve in water forming a neutral or very weakly acidic solution.

$$NaCl(s) + aq \longrightarrow Na^+(aq) + Cl^-(aq)$$
$$MgCl_2(s) + aq \longrightarrow Mg^{2+}(aq) + 2Cl^-(aq)$$

Reactions of non-metal chlorides

The covalent chlorides are *hydrolysed* by water forming a strongly acidic solution containing hydrochloric acid.

$$AlCl_3(s) + 3H_2O(l) \longrightarrow Al(OH)_3(s) + 3HCl(aq)$$
$$SiCl_4(l) + 2H_2O(l) \longrightarrow SiO_2(s) + 4HCl(aq)$$
$$PCl_5(s) + 4H_2O(l) \longrightarrow H_3PO_4(aq) + 5HCl(aq)$$

NaCl and $MgCl_2$ are white ionic compounds

$AlCl_3$ is a white covalent compound

PCl_5 and $SiCl_4$ are colourless covalent compounds

This periodicity of properties is repeated across each period

See also polarisation pp. 23–24

Trends in the s-block elements

The Group 1 elements and their compounds

Characteristic properties

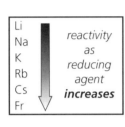

- The most reactive metal group, strong reducing agents.
- Soft metals.
- Low density: Li, Na and K all float on water.
- In reactions, the alkali metal is oxidised, losing one electron to form a 1+ ion: $M \longrightarrow M^+ + e^-$.
- Compounds are colourless.
- Reactivity increases down the group.

Reaction with oxygen

Vigorous reaction forming a mixture of metal oxides, including $(M^+)_2O^{2-}$ (white solids):
$$4Na(s) + O_2(g) \longrightarrow 2Na_2O(s).$$

Action of water

- Vigorous reaction giving an alkaline solution of metal hydroxide and hydrogen:
$2Na(s) + 2H_2O(l) \longrightarrow 2NaOH(aq) + H_2(g).$
- Reactivity increases down group reflecting the increasing ease of losing electrons.
- The ionisation energy of the metal is the most important factor in this process.

Trend in reactivity

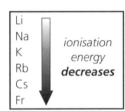

As the group is descended:
- atomic radius increases $\longrightarrow$ decrease in attraction
- number of inner shells increases $\longrightarrow$ shielding increases
- $\therefore$ ionisation energy decreases down the group
- it is easier to remove an electron and reactivity increases.

The Group 2 elements and their compounds

Reactive metals, although less reactive than those in Group 1.
In a typical reaction, the alkaline earth metal is oxidised, losing two electrons:
$M \longrightarrow M^{2+} + 2e^-$.

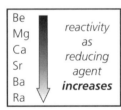

Reaction with oxygen

Vigorous reaction forming a metal oxide, $M^{2+}O^{2-}$ (white solid):
$2Ca(s) + O_2(g) \longrightarrow 2CaO(s).$

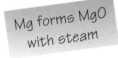

Mg forms MgO with steam

Action of water

- Vigorous reaction giving an alkaline solution of the metal hydroxide and hydrogen.
$Ca(s) + 2H_2O(l) \longrightarrow Ca(OH)_2(aq) + H_2(g).$
- Reactivity increases down group - increasing ease of losing electrons.
- Mg reacts very slowly with water but quickly with steam forming MgO:
$Mg(s) + H_2O(g) \longrightarrow MgO(s) + H_2(g).$

The thermal decomposition of the carbonates and nitrates

MgCO₃
CaCO₃
SrCO₃
BaCO₃

ease of thermal decomposition **decreases**

Heat decomposes Group 2 carbonates:

$$CaCO_3(s) \longrightarrow CaO(s) + CO_2(g).$$

- Ease of decomposition decreases down the group – related to polarising power of metal cation.

$MgCO_3$ decomposes with gentle heat:

Polarisation occurs when a small cation distorts the electron shells of a larger anion. The polarising effect is greatest between a small densely charged cation and a large anion

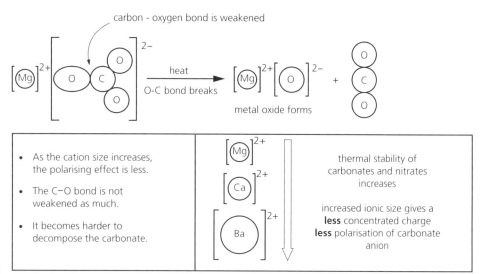

carbon - oxygen bond is weakened

heat
O-C bond breaks

metal oxide forms

- As the cation size increases, the polarising effect is less.
- The C–O bond is not weakened as much.
- It becomes harder to decompose the carbonate.

thermal stability of carbonates and nitrates increases

increased ionic size gives a **less** concentrated charge **less** polarisation of carbonate anion

A similar trend of the relative ease of decomposition occurs for the Group 2 nitrates:

$$Ca(NO_3)_2(s) \longrightarrow CaO(s) + 2NO_2(g) + \tfrac{1}{2}O_2(g)$$

The solubility of Group 2 sulphates

See also 'Enthalpy change of solution' pp.55

Solubility decreases down the group.
The trend is related to the relative magnitude of:

- lattice energy and
- hydration energy.

MgSO₄
CaSO₄
SrSO₄
BaSO₄

solubility **decreases**

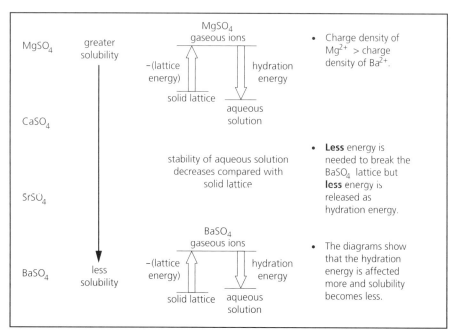

MgSO₄

greater solubility

MgSO₄ gaseous ions

–(lattice energy)   hydration energy

solid lattice

aqueous solution

- Charge density of Mg^{2+} > charge density of Ba^{2+}.

CaSO₄

stability of aqueous solution decreases compared with solid lattice

SrSO₄

- **Less** energy is needed to break the $BaSO_4$ lattice but **less** energy is released as hydration energy.

BaSO₄

less solubility

BaSO₄ gaseous ions

–(lattice energy)   hydration energy

solid lattice   aqueous solution

- The diagrams show that the hydration energy is affected more and solubility becomes less.

Trends in Group 7 – the halogens

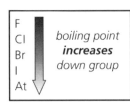

The halogens and their compounds

- Elements exist as diatomic molecules, X_2.
- Boiling point increases down the group
  – increased van der Waals' forces between molecules (from extra electrons).
- Reactive non-metals, strong oxidising agents.
- In a typical reaction, each halogen atom gains one electron:
  $$\tfrac{1}{2}X_2 + e^- \longrightarrow X^-.$$

The relative reactivity of the elements as oxidising agents

Demonstrated by displacement reactions in aqueous halides using Cl_2, Br_2 and I_2.
Chlorine oxidises both Br^- and I^-:
$$Cl_2(aq) + 2Br^-(aq) \longrightarrow 2Cl^-(aq) + Br_2(aq)$$
$$Cl_2(aq) + 2I^-(aq) \longrightarrow 2Cl^-(aq) + I_2(aq)$$

Bromine oxidises I^- only:
$$Br_2(aq) + 2I^-(aq) \longrightarrow 2Br^-(aq) + I_2(aq)$$

Iodine does not oxidise either Cl^- or Br^-.

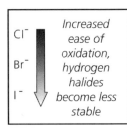

Testing for halide ions

Addition of aqueous silver ions followed by aqueous ammonia:

chloride:	$Ag^+(aq) + Cl^-(aq) \longrightarrow AgCl(s)$	*white precipitate, soluble in dilute $NH_3(aq)$*
bromide:	$Ag^+(aq) + Br^-(aq) \longrightarrow AgBr(s)$	*cream precipitate, soluble in conc $NH_3(aq)$*
iodide:	$Ag^+(aq) + I^-(aq) \longrightarrow AgI(s)$	*yellow precipitate, insoluble in conc $NH_3(aq)$*

Reaction of halides with concentrated sulphuric acid

NaCl: HCl forms - no oxidation:
$$NaCl \xrightarrow{H_2SO_4} HCl$$

NaBr: HBr forms with some oxidation to Br_2 – H_2SO_4 (+6) reduced to SO_2 (+4):
$$NaBr \xrightarrow{H_2SO_4} HBr \xrightarrow{H_2SO_4} Br_2 + SO_2$$

NaI: HI forms with almost all oxidised to I_2 - H_2SO_4 (+6) reduced to SO_2 (+4) and H_2S (–2):
$$NaI \xrightarrow{H_2SO_4} HI \xrightarrow{H_2SO_4} I_2 + SO_2 + H_2S$$

The reaction of chlorine with aqueous sodium hydroxide

Redox reactions: different products with different conditions:
cold: $Cl_2(aq) + 2NaOH(aq) \longrightarrow NaCl(aq) + NaClO(aq) + H_2O(l)$

$0 \longrightarrow -1$ *chlorine reduced*
$0 \longrightarrow +1$ *chlorine oxidised*

- Example of disproportionation: chlorine is both oxidised and reduced.

Further disproportionation in hot, concentrated NaOH (aq):
hot: $3NaClO (aq) \longrightarrow 2NaCl (aq) + NaClO_3 (aq)$

$+1 \longrightarrow -1$ *chlorine reduced*
$+1 \longrightarrow +5$ *chlorine oxidised*

The transition elements and the *d*-block elements ▪▪

Notice that the 4s electrons have already been added.
The 3d sub-shell is at a higher energy and is filled **after** the 4s sub-shell

d-block elements
The *d* sub-shell is filled across the *d*-block

| Sc | Ti | V | Cr | Mn | Fe | Co | Ni | Cu | Zn |

Transition elements

- The elements in the *d*-block, Ti–Cu, are transition elements:
- **A transition element has at least one ion with a partially filled *d* sub-shell**.
- BUT Sc and Zn are not 'transition elements' because they do not form an ion with a partially filled *d* sub-shell:
  Sc [Ar] $3d^1 4s^2$ ⟶ Sc^{3+} only   [Ar]   *3d empty*
  Zn [Ar] $3d^{10} 4s^2$ ⟶ Zn^{2+} only   [Ar] $3d^{10}$ *3d full*

Electronic configuration of the *d*-block elements

d sub-shell fills									
Sc [Ar] $3d^1 4s^2$	Ti [Ar] $3d^2 4s^2$	V [Ar] $3d^3 4s^2$	Cr [Ar] $3d^5 4s^1$	Mn [Ar] $3d^5 4s^2$	Fe [Ar] $3d^6 4s^2$	Co [Ar] $3d^7 4s^2$	Ni [Ar] $3d^8 4s^2$	Cu [Ar] $3d^{10} 4s^1$	Zn [Ar] $3d^{10} 4s^2$

Cr and Mn have a half-full d sub-shell of $3d^5$:
- chromium, Cr: [Ar] $3d^5 4s^1$
- manganese, Mn: [Ar] $3d^5 4s^2$
- each *d*-orbital contains only one electron

  $3d^5$ | ↑ | ↑ | ↑ | ↑ | ↑ |

- there is no repulsion between electrons in the same *d*-orbital
- the half-full *d* sub-shell gives stability.

Cu and Zn have a full d sub-shell of $3d^{10}$:
- copper, Cu: [Ar] $3d^{10}$ $4s^1$
- zinc,   Zn: [Ar] $3d^{10}$ $4s^2$
- all *d*-orbitals contain paired electrons

  $3d^{10}$ | ↑↓ | ↑↓ | ↑↓ | ↑↓ | ↑↓ |

- the full *d* sub-shell gives stability.

See also the stability from a half-full p sub-shell pp. 18

It is easy to work out the electronic configuration of any of the *d*-block elements Sc-Zn provided you take account of the factors above.

Typical properties of the transition elements

- hard, dense metals
- many are catalysts
- form coloured compounds and ions
- high melting and boiling points
- form a variety of oxidation states
- form complex ions with ligands

Physical properties
These elements have the usual properties of a metal and also have
- a high density: the atoms are small and pack closely together
- a high boiling point: strong forces between atoms.

Formation of *d*-block ions

The 4*s* and 3*d* energy levels are very close together and electrons can be lost from both of these sub-shells to form positive ions.

Many of the *d*-block elements can form more than one ion with different oxidation states. These ions form by the loss of:

- the 4*s* electrons first
- different numbers of 3*d* electrons.

Example The formation of Fe^{2+} and Fe^{3+} ions from Fe

When forming ions, the 4s electrons are lost first, **before** the 3d electrons

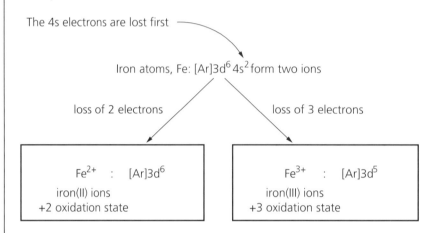

The 4s electrons are lost first

Iron atoms, Fe: $[Ar]3d^6 4s^2$ form two ions

loss of 2 electrons

loss of 3 electrons

Fe^{2+} : $[Ar]3d^6$
iron(II) ions
+2 oxidation state

Fe^{3+} : $[Ar]3d^5$
iron(III) ions
+3 oxidation state

Common oxidation states of d-block ions

The common oxidation states of *d*-block ions are shown below. The colours are those of aqueous solutions.

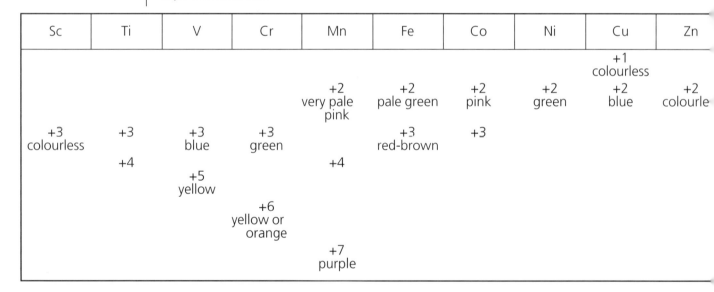

Sc	Ti	V	Cr	Mn	Fe	Co	Ni	Cu	Zn
								+1 colourless	
				+2 very pale pink	+2 pale green	+2 pink	+2 green	+2 blue	+2 colourless
+3 colourless	+3	+3 blue	+3 green		+3 red-brown	+3			
	+4			+4					
		+5 yellow							
			+6 yellow or orange						
				+7 purple					

Transition metal ions and colour

Only those ions that have a partially filled d sub-shell are coloured

Colour is caused when an electron is transferred within the *d* sub-shell.
Copper: $[Ar]3d^{10}4s^1$ forms two ions, Cu^+: $[Ar]3d^{10}$ and Cu^{2+}: $[Ar]3d^9$

The Cu^{2+} ion is coloured because:
- the *d* sub-shell is partially full, $[Ar]3d^9$, allowing electron transfer:

[Ar] $3d^9$ | ↑↓ | ↑↓ | ↑↓ | ↑↓ | ↑ | electron transfer possible, causes colour by absorption of radiation

The Cu^+ ion is uncoloured because:
- the *d* sub-shell is full, $[Ar]3d^{10}$, preventing electron transfer:

[Ar] $3d^{10}$ | ↑↓ | ↑↓ | ↑↓ | ↑↓ | ↑↓ | no electron transfer possible - no colour.

Transition elements as catalysts

The catalytic properties of transition elements are often used in industrial processes.
Iron is a catalyst used in the Haber Process to make ammonia.
Vanadium as V_2O_5 is used in the Contact Process to make sulphuric acid.
Pd, Pt, Rh and Au are used in the catalytic converters found in car exhaust systems.
Pt, Pd and Ni are used in reactions involving hydrogen, such as the preparation of margarine from vegetable oils.

Transition element complexes

See also
Equilibria,
rates and
industrial
processes
pp. 61

Transition metal ions are small and densely charged. They strongly attract electron-rich species with lone pairs of electrons called *ligands* forming complex ions.

A **ligand** is an atom or ion that:
- donates a lone pair of electrons
- forms a coordinate (dative covalent) bond with a small metal ion.

Common ligands include: H_2O, Cl^-, NH_3, CN^-.

A **complex ion** forms when ligands surround a metal ion, forming coordinate bonds to it.

A ligand has a
lone pair of
electrons

Example Complex ions of Cu^{2+}
The number of ligands that bond to the central metal ion depends on electronic configuration and size.

The size of a
ligand helps to
decide the
geometry of
the complex
ion

The hexaaquacopper(II) complex ion
- Six H_2O ligands bond to the central Cu^{2+} ion to form the complex ion, $[Cu(H_2O)_6]^{2+}$.
- The 6 electron pairs arrange themselves so that they are as far apart as possible forming an **octahedral** shape.

$[Cu(H_2O)_6]^{2+}$
octahedral
6 coordinate

The tetrachlorocopper(II) complex ion
- Compared with NH_3 and H_2O, the larger Cl^- ions interact differently with the metal ion forming a tetrahedral complex ion.

$[CuCl_4]^{2-}$
tetrahedral
4 coordinate

General rules for complex ions
Although there are exceptions, the following general rules are useful.
- Complex ions involving water and ammonia ligands are usually 6–coordinate and octahedral.
- Complex ions involving chloride ligands are usually 4–coordinate and tetrahedral.

Typical formulae are:

metal ion	M^{2+}	M^{3+}
complex with H_2O	$[M(H_2O)_6]^{2+}$	$[M(H_2O)_6]^{3+}$
complex with NH_3	$[M(NH_3)_6]^{2+}$	$[M(NH_3)_6]^{3+}$
complex with Cl^-	$[MCl_4]^{2-}$	$[MCl_4]^-$

Common exceptions
- With NH_3, Cu^{2+}(aq) forms the mixed complex ion: $[Cu(NH_3)_4(H_2O)_2]^{2+}$.
- Ag^+ forms linear complexes that are 2-coordinate, e.g. $[Ag(H_2O)_2]^+$, $[Ag(NH_3)_2]^+$ and $[AgCl_2]^-$.

Ag+ complexes
are colourless
– the 4d
sub-shell is full

Reactions of transition metal ions

Main types of reaction:
- ligand exchange
- redox reactions
- precipitation.

Ligand exchange reactions of complex ions

A ligand may substitute for another ligand in the complex ion. This *ligand exchange* will often produce a change in colour.

Example Exchange of $4H_2O$ molecules in $[Cu(H_2O)_6]^{2+}$ by $4NH_3$ molecules.

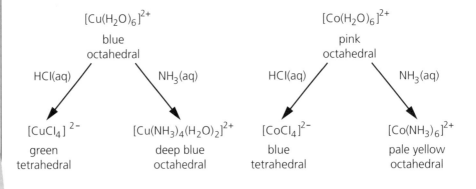

pale-blue solution
$[Cu(H_2O)_6]^{2+}$ + $4\ddot{N}H_3$ $\longrightarrow$ $[Cu(NH_3)_4(H_2O)_2]^{2+}$ + $4H_2\ddot{O}$

deep-blue solution

Ligand substitution reactions of copper and cobalt

$[Cu(H_2O)_6]^{2+}$
blue
octahedral

HCl(aq)   NH$_3$(aq)

$[CuCl_4]^{2-}$ $[Cu(NH_3)_4(H_2O)_2]^{2+}$
green   deep blue
tetrahedral   octahedral

$[Co(H_2O)_6]^{2+}$
pink
octahedral

HCl(aq)   NH$_3$(aq)

$[CoCl_4]^{2-}$ $[Co(NH_3)_6]^{2+}$
blue   pale yellow
tetrahedral   octahedral

In the reactions above:
- concentrated hydrochloric acid is used as a source of the ligand, Cl^-
- concentrated aqueous ammonia is used as a source of the ligand, NH_3.

The $[Co(NH_3)_6]^{2+}$ ion slowly oxidises and darkens in air to form $[Co(NH_3)_6]^{3+}$

Using colours for chemical tests

The characteristic colour of a complex ion can often be used as an identification test in chemical analysis.

Example The thiocyanate ion, CNS^-, produces a deep-red colour with Fe^{3+} ions by ligand exchange.

$[Fe(H_2O)_6]^{3+}$ + $:SCN^-$ $\longrightarrow$ $[Fe(H_2O)_5(SCN)]^{2+}$ + H_2O
pale red-brown solution   deep blood-red solution

Redox reactions of transition metal ions

Many redox reactions take place in which transition metals change their oxidation state by **gaining** or **losing** electrons.

Using Fe²⁺ ions as a reducing agent

Reaction with acidified MnO_4^- ions:

See also Redox
pp. 79–83

oxidation:	$Fe^{2+}(aq) \longrightarrow Fe^{3+}(aq) + e^-$	
	+2 $\qquad$ +3	
reduction:	$MnO_4^-(aq) + 8H^+(aq) + 5e^- \longrightarrow Mn^{2+}(aq) + 4H_2O(l)$	
	+7 $\qquad\qquad\qquad\qquad$ +2	

To give the overall equation:

balance:	$5Fe^{2+}(aq) \longrightarrow 5Fe^{3+}(aq) + 5e^-$
	$MnO_4^-(aq) + 8H^+(aq) + 5e^- \longrightarrow Mn^{2+}(aq) + 4H_2O(l)$
add half equations:	
	$5Fe^{2+}(aq) + MnO_4^-(aq) + 8H^+(aq) \longrightarrow Mn^{2+}(aq) + 4H_2O(l) + 5Fe^{3+}(aq)$

Reaction with acidified $Cr_2O_7^{2-}$ ions:

oxidation:	$Fe^{2+}(aq) \longrightarrow Fe^{3+}(aq) + e^-$
	+2 $\qquad$ +3
reduction:	$Cr_2O_7^{2-}(aq) + 14H^+(aq) + 6e^- \longrightarrow 2Cr^{3+}(aq) + 7H_2O(l)$
	+6 $\qquad\qquad\qquad\qquad$ +3
overall equation:	
	$6Fe^{2+}(aq) + Cr_2O_7^{2-}(aq) + 14H^+(aq) \longrightarrow 2Cr^{3+}(aq) + 7H_2O(l) + 6Fe^{3+}(aq)$

Redox reactions involving Fe²⁺ (aq) are often used in titrations with oxidising agents such as MnO₄²⁻ (aq) and Cr₂O₇²⁻ (aq)

Other redox reactions

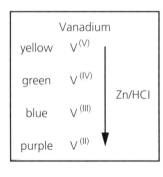

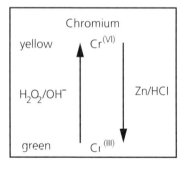

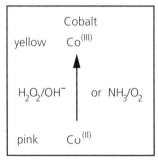

Notes

Check your A-level syllabus to see if you need to learn these extra redox reactions

For moving *up* oxidation states, H_2O_2/OH^- is a good general oxidising agent.	For moving *down* oxidation states, Zn/HCl is a good general reducing agent.

Chromate(VI) ions and dichromate(VI) ions
These two forms exist at different pH values:

$$2H^+ + 2CrO_4^{2-} \underset{OH^-}{\overset{H^+}{\rightleftharpoons}} Cr_2O_7^{2-} + H_2O$$
$$\text{yellow} \qquad\qquad\qquad \text{orange}$$

exists in *ALKALI*		exists in *ACID*

Precipitation reactions

You should be able to construct a balanced equation for any precipitation reaction.

Acidity of transition metal ions

- Transition metal ions behave as weak acids in aqueous solution.
- The small cation polarises water ligands, causing loss of a proton.
- This is more marked with a 3+ cation with its greater charge/size ratio than with a 2+ cation:

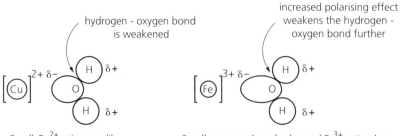

Small Cu^{2+} cation readily polarises the water ligand

Smaller, more densely charged Fe^{3+} cation has a greater charge/size ratio: increased polarisation

$[Cu(H_2O)_6]^{2+} + H_2O \rightleftharpoons [Cu(H_2O)_5(OH)]^+ + H_3O^+$ $\qquad$ very weakly acidic

$[Fe(H_2O)_6]^{3+} + H_2O \rightleftharpoons [Fe(H_2O)_5(OH)]^{2+} + H_3O^+$ $\qquad$ weakly acidic

Precipitation reactions

- Addition of aqueous alkali causes further removal of protons resulting in a hydrated hydroxide precipitate. Suitable sources of hydroxide are NaOH(aq) or aqueous ammonia, NH_3(aq).

$$[Cr(H_2O)_6]^{3+}(aq) + 3OH^-(aq) \rightleftharpoons Cr(H_2O)_3(OH)_3(s) + 3H_2O(l)$$
$$\text{(green-grey precipitate)}$$

Note that the precipitate has no charge.

- Further addition of aqueous alkali such as NaOH(aq) may cause the precipitate to dissolve forming a further complex:

$$Cr(H_2O)_3(OH)_3(s) + OH^-(aq) \rightleftharpoons [Cr(H_2O)_4]^-(aq) + 3H_2O(l)$$
$$\text{(green solution)}$$

- If ammonia is used as the source of OH⁻, then excess ammonia usually results in ligand exchange:

$$Cr(H_2O)_3(OH)_3(s) + 6NH_3(aq) \rightleftharpoons [Cr(NH_3)_6]^{3+}(aq) + 3H_2O(l) + 3OH^-(aq)$$
$$\text{(green solution)}$$

Summary of important precipitations
There is no substitute here for memorising the reactions.
General rules to help are:

- aqueous alkali produces a hydrated hydroxide precipitate with no overall charge
- excess NaOH(aq) *may* cause the precipitate to dissolve as a further complex forms; this is more likely to occur with M^{3+}(aq) ions than with the less acidic M^{2+}(aq) ions
- excess NH_3(aq) *usually* causes the precipitate to dissolve by ligand exchange; this *usually* results in a complex ion of the type $[M(NH_3)_6]^{3+}$.

5 Chemical energetics

Enthalpy

Enthalpy, *H*, is the *heat energy* that is stored in a chemical system.
Enthalpy cannot be measured experimentally but an **enthalpy change** can be measured from the temperature change in a chemical reaction.

> **An enthalpy change**, Δ*H*, is the heat energy exchange with the surroundings at constant pressure.
> **The first law of thermodynamics** states that energy may be exchanged between reactants and the surroundings but the *total* energy remains constant.

Exothermic reactions

During the chemical reaction, heat energy is **released** to the surroundings.
Any energy **loss** from the chemicals provides the same energy **gain** to the surroundings.

Energy pathway diagram (reaction profile)

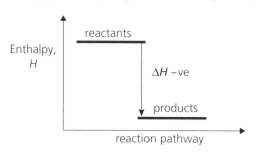

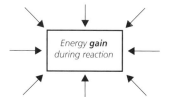

Energy gain by the surroundings
(identified by a temperature **rise** Δ*T*)

In an exothermic reaction:
- heat is given out (temperature rise to the surroundings)
- chemicals lose energy
- Δ*H* is negative.

Endothermic reactions

During the chemical reaction, heat energy is **taken** in from the surroundings.
Any energy **gain** to the chemicals provides the same energy **loss** from the surroundings.

Energy pathway diagram (reaction profile)

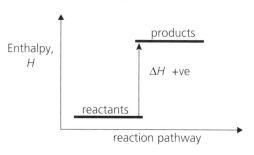

Energy loss from the surroundings
(identified by a temperature **fall** Δ*T*)

In an endothermic reaction:
- heat is taken in (temperature fall to the surroundings)
- chemicals gain energy
- Δ*H* is positive.

Bond breaking
requires energy:
ENDOTHERMIC

Bond making
releases
energy:
EXOTHERMIC

See also
'Activation
energy', pp. 49

Bond energies
are positive
and refer to
bond breaking

Not all C–H
bonds are
created equal

The relative
strengths
between the
bonds in the
reactants and
the bonds in
the products
decide whether
a reaction is
exothermic or
endothermic

Bond making and bond breaking

Bond breaking is an endothermic process and **requires** energy.
Bond making is an exothermic process and **releases** energy. Bond making produces a **greater** stability and a **lower** energy state.

During every chemical reaction:
- energy is first needed to break bonds
- energy is then released as new bonds are formed.

Bond energy

Enthalpy is stored within chemical bonds. **Bond energy** provides an indication of the strength of a chemical bond.

> The **bond energy** or **bond energy term** is the enthalpy change required to **break** and separate **1 mole of bonds** so that the resulting gaseous species exert no forces upon each other.

Bond dissociation energy

Although typical bond energies can be tabulated, each bond is slightly different. The **actual** energy of a particular bond in a chemical is referred to as the **bond dissociation energy**.

> **Bond dissociation energy** is the enthalpy change required to break and separate 1 mole of a particular bond.
> E.g. The C–H bonds in methane CH_4 and in chloromethane CH_3Cl are in different environments and they will have different bond energies.
>
> The Cl atom in CH_3Cl affects the environment of the C–H bonds.
>
>
> C–H bonds have a different strength and a different bond energy

It is the **average** bond energy that is listed in data books. This is useful as an indication of the strength of a *typical* bond.
The *average* bond energy for the C–H bond is $+413$ kJ mol^{-1}.

Using bond energies to determine enthalpy changes

Enthalpy change = Σ(bond energies of reactants) $-\Sigma$ (bond energies of products)
For the reaction:

$$CH_4(g) \quad + \quad 2O_2(g) \longrightarrow CO_2(g) \quad + \quad 2H_2O(g)$$

Average bond energies: C–H, $+413$ kJ mol^{-1}; C=O, $+740$ kJ mol^{-1}
O=O, $+497$ kJ mol^{-1}; O–H, $+463$ kJ mol^{-1}

Bonds broken: 4(C–H) + 2(O=O)	Bonds made: 2(C=O) + 4(O–H)
$\Delta H = \{ (4 \times 413) + (2 \times 497) \}$ kJ mol^{-1}	$\Delta H = - \{(2 \times 740) + (4 \times 463)\}$ kJ mol^{-1}
(endothermic)	*(exothermic)*

Enthalpy change: $= \{ (4 \times 413) + (2 \times 497) \} - \{ (2 \times 740) + (4 \times 463) \}$ kJ mol^{-1}
$= -\mathbf{686}$ kJ mol^{-1}

Standard enthalpy changes

$\Delta H^{\ominus}$ refers to an enthalpy change under standard conditions.
Standard conditions are:

- a pressure of 100 kPa (1 atmosphere)
- a temperature of 298K (25°C) (other standard temperatures are sometimes used)
- a concentration of 1 mol dm^{-3} (for aqueous solutions).

A **standard state** is the physical state of a substance under standard conditions. The standard state of water at 298 K and 100 kPa is a liquid.

Standard pressure is shown differently in different books: as 100 kPa or 101 kPa or 1 bar or 1 atmosphere

Standard enthalpy change of reaction

> The **standard enthalpy change of reaction** $\Delta H_r^{\ominus}$ is the enthalpy change that accompanies a reaction in the quantities that are expressed in a chemical equation under standard conditions.

Always use a chemical equation or an unambiguous definition with a stated enthalpy change

- The enthalpy change of reaction depends on the quantities shown in a chemical equation and so it is important always to quote this value with an equation.

For the reaction:

$$H_2(g) + \tfrac{1}{2}O_2(g) \longrightarrow H_2O(l) \qquad \Delta H_r^{\ominus} = -286 \text{ kJ mol}^{-1}$$
$$1 \text{ mol} \quad \tfrac{1}{2}\text{mol} \qquad 1 \text{ mol}$$

but with twice the quantities, there is twice the enthalpy change:

$$2H_2(g) + O_2(g) \longrightarrow 2H_2O(l) \qquad \Delta H_r^{\ominus} = -572 \text{ kJ mol}^{-1}$$
$$2 \text{ mol} \quad 1 \text{ mol} \qquad 2 \text{ mol}$$

Standard enthalpy change of combustion

$\Delta H_r^{\ominus}$ has units of kJ mol^{-1}
The mol^{-1} means 'for the number of moles shown in the equation'

> **The standard enthalpy change of combustion** $\Delta H_c^{\ominus}$ is the enthalpy change that takes place when one mole of a substance reacts completely with oxygen under standard conditions.

Example $C_2H_4(g) + 3O_2(g) \longrightarrow 2CO_2(g) + 2H_2O(l)$ $\qquad \Delta H_c^{\ominus} = -1411 \text{ kJ mol}^{-1}$

- Complete **combustion of 1 mole** of $C_2H_4(g)$ releases 1411 kJ of heat energy to the surroundings at 298 K and 100 kPa.

Standard enthalpy change of formation

> **The standard enthalpy change of formation** $\Delta H_f^{\ominus}$ is the enthalpy change that takes place when one mole of a compound is formed from its constituent elements in their standard states under standard conditions.

The standard enthalpy change of formation of an element is defined as zero.
The 'formation' of $H_2(g)$ from $H_2(g)$ involves no chemical change so there will be no enthalpy change

Example $H_2(g) + \tfrac{1}{2}O_2(g) \longrightarrow H_2O(l)$ $\qquad \Delta H_f^{\ominus} = -286 \text{ kJ mol}^{-1}$

The **formation of 1 mole** of $H_2O(l)$ from $H_2(g)$ and $O_2(g)$ releases 286 kJ of heat energy to the surroundings at 298 K and 100 kPa.

Standard enthalpy change of neutralisation

> The **enthalpy change of neutralisation** $\Delta H_n^{\ominus}$ is the energy change that accompanies the neutralisation of 1 mole of $H^+(aq)$ from an acid by 1 mole of $OH^-(aq)$ from an alkali to form 1 mole of $H_2O(l)$.

Example $H^+(aq) + OH^-(aq) \longrightarrow H_2O(l)$ $\qquad \Delta H_n^{\ominus} = -57.1 \text{ kJ mol}^{-1}$
$$1 \text{ mol} \quad 1 \text{ mol} \qquad 1 \text{ mol}$$

Direct determination of enthalpy changes

The *energy* change, Q, to the surroundings can be calculated using the relationship:

$$Q = m \, c \, \Delta T \text{ Joules}$$

- *m* is the *mass* of the surroundings that experience a temperature change.
- *c* is the *specific heat capacity* of the surroundings.
- ΔT is the *temperature change* (final temperature – initial temperature) of the surroundings.

The specific heat capacity of a substance is the energy required to raise the temperature of 1 g of the substance by 1°C

Example 1
Addition of 1.60 g (an excess) of magnesium to 100 cm³ of 2.00 mol dm⁻³ CuSO₄(aq) raised the temperature from 20°C to 65.0°C. Find the enthalpy change for the reaction:

$$Mg(s) + CuSO_4(aq) \longrightarrow MgSO_4(aq) + Cu(s)$$

specific heat capacity *c*, of solution, = 4.18 J g⁻¹ K⁻¹; density of solution = 1.00 g cm⁻³

Find the energy change:

> 100 cm³ of solution has a mass of 100 g; $\Delta T = 45.0°C$
> Energy **gain** to surroundings, $Q = m \, c \, \Delta T = 100 \times 4.18 \times 45.0$ J = **+18810 J**
> ∴ Energy **loss** from chemicals = **−18810 J**

Any energy gain by the surroundings must have come from the same energy loss in the chemical reaction

Find how many moles reacted:

> Number of moles of CuSO₄ that reacted $= \dfrac{2.00 \times 100}{1000}$ mol = 0.200 mol

Scale the quantities to those in the equation:

> $Mg(s) + CuSO_4(aq) \longrightarrow MgSO_4(aq) + Cu(s)$
> 1 mol   1 mol   1 mol   1 mol
>   0.200 mol (1/5th mol) of CuSO₄ reacts to produce an ΔH of −18810 J
>   ∴ 1 mol of CuSO₄ reacts to produce an ΔH of 5 × −18800 J = −94050 J

Assume that solids, such as Mg (s) make little difference to the energy change

∴ *Enthalpy change of reaction is given by:*

> $Mg(s) + CuSO_4(aq) \longrightarrow MgSO_4(aq) + Cu(s)$ $\Delta H = -94.1$ kJ mol⁻¹
> *(to 3 significant figures)*

Example 2
The complete combustion of 1.60 g of methane, CH₄, heated 300 cm³ of water by 70.0°C. Find the enthalpy change of combustion of methane assuming that all of the heat energy was taken in by the water.

Find the energy change:

> Energy **gain** by surroundings, $Q = m \, c \, \Delta T = 300 \times 4.18 \times 70.0$ J = **+87780 J**
> ∴ Energy **loss** from chemicals = **−87780 J**

Find how many moles reacted:

> 1.60 g of methane contains 1.60/16.0 mol = 0.100 mol CH₄

Scale the quantities for the combustion of 1 mole:

> 0.100 mol of CH₄ ⇨ − 87780 J
> ∴ 1 mol of CH₄ ⇨ − 10 × 87780 J
> ∴ $\Delta H_c^{\ominus}$ (CH₄) = −877800 J = −878 kJ mol⁻¹ *(to 3 significant figures)*

The feasibility of a chemical reaction

The value of an enthalpy change only provides a guide to *stability* and the *feasibility* of a reaction.

It does not indicate:
- whether the reaction will actually occur
- the rate of the reaction.

For example, sucrose is oxidised by oxygen in a highly exothermic reaction:

$$C_{12}H_{22}O_{11}(s) + 12O_2(g) \longrightarrow 12CO_2(g) + 11H_2O(g) \quad \Delta H = -5644 \text{ kJ mol}^{-1}$$

- The reaction is *very likely* to take place because of the great amount of energy released in this reaction.
- However, the reaction does not take place spontaneously at room temperature.
- Before a reaction can take place, activation energy must be put into the system, perhaps from an external heat source.

> The **activation energy** of a reaction is the energy required to start a reaction by the breaking of bonds.
> Activation energy is often supplied by a spark or by heating the reactants.
> A large activation energy may 'protect' the reactants from taking part in the reaction (at room temperature).

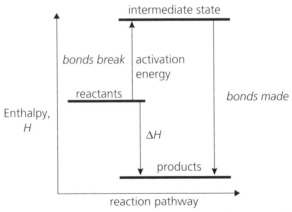

Activation energy and reaction mechanisms are discussed in more detail in the Reaction rates section

- The chemical equation gives no indication of the course of the reaction.

Although a chemical equation can sum up the starting and finishing situations, it provides no information about the reaction *pathway* or *mechanism*. Many reactions proceed via many steps, each with its own activation energy and ΔH value. Any step with a large energy barrier will hinder and **slow down** the progress of the reaction.

Indirect determination of enthalpy changes

Hess's Law

The enthalpy changes of many reactions cannot be found directly by carrying out an experiment. Hess's Law provides a method for the **indirect** determination of enthalpy changes.

Hess's Law is an extension of the First Law of Thermodynamics.

> **Hess's Law** states that, if a reaction can take place by more than one route and the initial and final conditions are the same, the total enthalpy change is the same for each route.

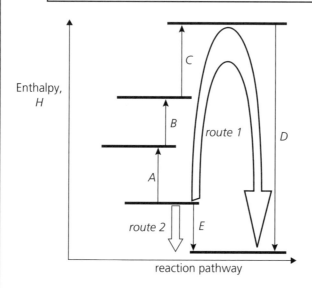

The reactants can be converted into the products by two alternative routes:

- *route 1*   A + B + C + D
- *route 2*   E

By Hess's Law, the total enthalpy change is the same for each route.

∴ A + B + C + D = E

Any of the enthalpy changes A-E can be determined provided that four of the enthalpy changes A-E are known.

Using standard enthalpy changes of combustion

Known enthalpy changes of combustion are used as a link between the reactants and the products to construct an *energy cycle:*

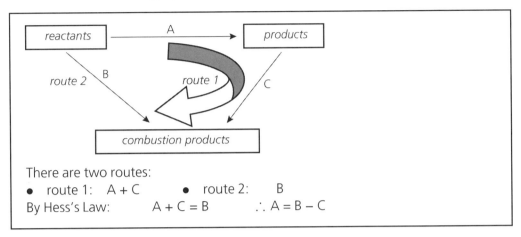

There are two routes:
- route 1:   A + C
- route 2:   B

By Hess's Law: A + C = B   ∴ A = B – C

Example
Find the enthalpy change for the reaction:

$$C(s) + 2H_2(g) \longrightarrow CH_4(g)$$

substance	$\Delta H_c^{\ominus}$ / kJ mol^{-1}
$C(s)$	−393.5
$H_2(g)$	−285.8
$CH_4(g)$	−890.3

Use enthalpy changes of combustion as a 'link' to construct an energy cycle:

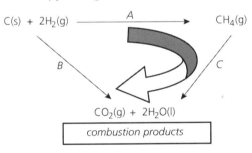

Add $\Delta H_c^{\ominus}$ data to the energy cycle:

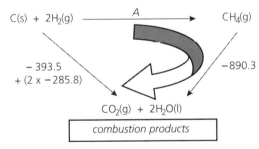

Calculate the unknown enthalpy change:

By Hess's Law, A + C = B
  ∴ A = B – C
  ∴ A = [(−393.5) + (2 × −285.8)] – [(−890.3)]

  underbrace: B   C

  ∴   Enthalpy change A = **−74.8 kJ mol^{-1}**
  ∴ $C(s) + 2H_2(g) \longrightarrow CH_4(g)$ $\Delta H^{\ominus} = -74.8$ kJ mol^{-1}

Using standard enthalpy changes of formation

Known enthalpy changes of formation are used as a link between the reactants and the products to construct an *energy cycle*.

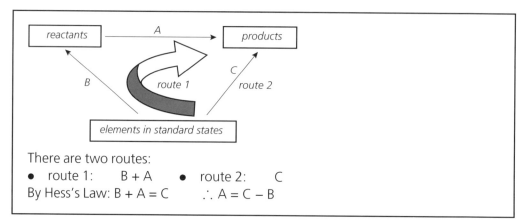

There are two routes:
- route 1:   B + A
- route 2:   C

By Hess's Law: B + A = C   ∴ A = C − B

Example

Find the enthalpy change for the reaction:

$$C_2H_6(g) + 3\tfrac{1}{2}O_2(g) \longrightarrow 2CO_2(g) + 3H_2O(l)$$

substance	$\Delta H_f^\ominus$ / kJ mol⁻¹
C_2H_6 (g)	−84.6
CO_2 (g)	−393.7
H_2O (l)	−285.8

Use enthalpy changes of formation as a 'link' to construct an energy cycle:

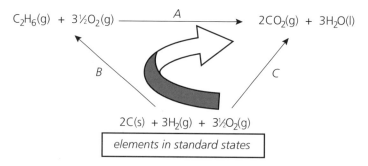

Add $\Delta H_f^\ominus$ data to the energy cycle:

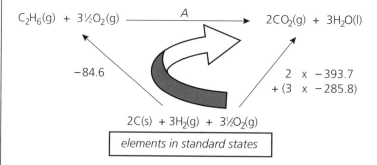

Calculate the unknown enthalpy change:

By Hess's Law, B + A = C

∴ A = C − B

∴ A = [(2 × −393.7) + (3 × −285.8)]− [(−84.6)]

                        C   B

∴ Enthalpy change A = −1560.2 kJ mol⁻¹

$C_2H_6(g) + 3\tfrac{1}{2}O_2(g) \longrightarrow 2CO_2(g) + 3H_2O(l)$: $\Delta H = -1560.2$ kJ mol⁻¹

The Born-Haber cycle

The Born-Haber cycle is an energy cycle involving the formation of an ionic lattice from elements in their standard states.

Definitions related to formation of an ionic lattice

Changes of state

> ***The standard enthalpy change of atomisation***, $(\Delta H_{at}{}^{\ominus})$ is the enthalpy change that accompanies the formation of **1** mole of gaseous atoms from an element in its standard state.
>
> $Na(s) \longrightarrow Na(g)$

> ***The standard enthalpy change of sublimation*** is the enthalpy change that accompanies the formation of **1** mole of gaseous atoms from a solid element in its standard state.
>
> $Na(s) \longrightarrow Na(g)$

> ***The standard enthalpy change of fusion*** is the enthalpy change that accompanies the change in state from a solid to a liquid of **1** mole of a substance at its melting point and 100 kPa (1 atmosphere pressure).
>
> $Na(s) \longrightarrow Na(l)$

> ***The standard enthalpy change of vaporisation*** or ***evaporation*** is the enthalpy change that accompanies the change in state from a liquid to a gas of **1** mole of a substance at its boiling point and 100 kPa (1 atmosphere pressure).
>
> $Na(l) \longrightarrow Na(g)$

Formation of ions

> ***The first electron affinity*** $(\Delta H_{E.A.}{}^{\ominus})$ is the enthalpy change that accompanies the **addition** of 1 electron to each atom in **1** mole of gaseous atoms to form **1** mole of gaseous 1– ions.
>
> $Cl(g) + e^- \longrightarrow Cl^-(g)$

> ***The first ionisation energy*** $(\Delta H_{I.E.}{}^{\ominus})$ is the enthalpy change that accompanies the **removal** of 1 electron from each atom in **1** mole of gaseous atoms to form **1** mole of gaseous 1+ ions.
>
> $Na(g) \longrightarrow Na^+(g) + e^-$

Formation of an ionic lattice

> ***The lattice energy*** $(\Delta H_{L.E.}{}^{\ominus})$ is the enthalpy change that accompanies the formation of **1** mole of an ionic compound from its constituent gaseous ions. $(\Delta H_{L.E.}{}^{\ominus}$ is exothermic.)
>
> $Na^+(g) + Cl^-(g) \longrightarrow Na^+Cl^-(s)$

Be careful when using ΔH_{at} involving diatomic elements. ΔH_{at} relates to the formation of 1 mole of atoms. For chlorine, this means $\frac{1}{2}Cl_2(g) \rightarrow Cl(g)$

For solid elements, this is identical to the standard enthalpy change of atomisation

Electron affinity is another enthalpy change of which to be careful. $\Delta H_{E.A.}{}^{\ominus}$ relates to the formation of 1 mole of 1– ions. For chlorine, this involves $Cl(g)$ only

Some Exam Boards use an alternative definition of lattice energy which is the reverse of the reaction shown. This gives an endothermic lattice energy

The Born-Haber cycle for the formation of an ionic lattice

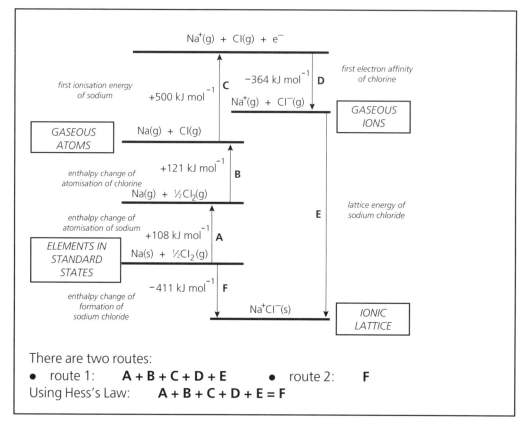

There are two routes:
- route 1:   **A + B + C + D + E**   • route 2:   **F**
Using Hess's Law: **A + B + C + D + E = F**

To determine the lattice energy of $Na^+Cl^-(s)$, **E**:
$\Delta H_{at}^{\ominus}\{Na(g)\} + \Delta H_{at}^{\ominus}\{Cl(g)\} + \Delta H_{I.E.}^{\ominus}\{Na(g)\} + \Delta H_{E.A.}^{\ominus}\{Cl(g)\} + \mathbf{E}$ = $\Delta H_f^{\ominus}\{Na^+Cl^-(s)\}$
$\therefore$ $108 + 121 + 500 + (-364) + \mathbf{E}$ $= -411$

Hence, the lattice energy of Na^+Cl^- (s), **E = −776** kJ mol⁻¹

Factors affecting the magnitude of lattice energy

Effect of ionic size

compound	lattice energy /kJ mol⁻¹	ions	effect of size
NaCl	−776	(+)(−)	ionic size increases:
NaBr	−742	(+)(−)	• greater distance between centres of ions
			• attraction between ions decreases
NaI	−705	(+)(−)	• lattice energy becomes less negative.

Effect of ionic charge

With increased charge on cation, two factors increase the magnitude of lattice energy:	$Na^+ \longrightarrow Mg^{2+}$ (+) (2+) increased charge $\longrightarrow$ greater attraction decreasing size $\longrightarrow$ greater attraction
With increased charge on anion, two competing factors:	$Cl^- \longrightarrow O^{2-}$ (1−) (2−) increased charge $\longrightarrow$ greater attraction increased size $\longrightarrow$ less attraction

Energy cycle for the formation of an aqueous solution

Definitions

> **The standard enthalpy change of solution** is the enthalpy change that accompanies the dissolving of 1 mole of a solute in a solvent to form an infinitely dilute solution under standard conditions.
>
> $$Na^+Cl^-(s) + aq \longrightarrow Na^+(aq) + Cl^-(aq)$$

> **The standard enthalpy change of hydration**, $\Delta H_{hyd}{}^{\ominus}$, of an ion is the enthalpy change that accompanies the hydration of **1 mole** of gaseous ions to form 1 mole of hydrated ions in an infinitely dilute solution under standard conditions.
>
> $$Na^+(g) + aq \longrightarrow Na^+(aq); \quad Cl^-(g) + aq \longrightarrow Cl^-(aq)$$

Energy cycle

Again, we have the conflict between the lattice energy definition used by different Exam Boards. For the endothermic definition used by some Exam boards, the energy change A would be labelled as +(lattice energy): +776 kJ mol⁻¹. Both methods give the same calculated value for the enthalpy change of solution

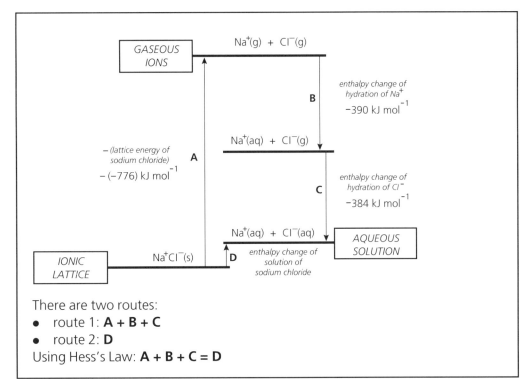

There are two routes:
- route 1: **A + B + C**
- route 2: **D**

Using Hess's Law: **A + B + C = D**

To determine the enthalpy change of solution of Na⁺Cl⁻(s), **D**:

$$-\Delta H_{L.E.}{}^{\ominus}\{NaCl(s)\} + \Delta H_{hyd}{}^{\ominus}\{Na^+(g)\} + \Delta H_{hyd}{}^{\ominus}\{Cl^-(g)\} = D$$

$$\therefore D = -(-776) + (-390) + (-384)$$

Hence, the enthalpy change of solution of Na⁺Cl⁻(s), **D = +2** kJ mol⁻¹

Hydrated ions

The values obtained for each ion depend upon the size of the charge and the size of the ion (see also pp. 44)

ion	Na⁺	Mg²⁺	Al³⁺	Cl⁻	Br⁻	I⁻
$\Delta H_{hyd}{}^{\ominus}$/kJ mol⁻¹	−390	−1891	−4613	−384	−351	−307
effect of charge	increasing ionic charge greater attraction for water					
ionic radius / nm	0.098	0.065	0.045	0.181	0.196	0.219
effect of size	decreasing ionic size greater attraction for water			increasing ionic size less attraction for water		

6 Equilibria

Reversible reactions

Dynamic equilibrium

Many reactions are **reversible**: they can take place in either direction.
At the equilibrium point:

- although there is no apparent change, both forward and reverse processes continue to take place
- the forward reaction proceeds at the same rate as the reverse reaction
- the concentrations of reactants and products are constant.

The equilibrium position:

- can be reached from either forward or reverse directions
- can only be achieved in a closed system
- can be changed by altering temperature, pressure or concentration.

Example
Equilibrium can exist between a partially soluble salt and its solution:

$AgCl(s) \rightleftharpoons Ag^+(aq) + Cl^-(aq)$

> In a chemical equation, reactants are on the left-hand side; products are on the right-hand side.
> A reversible reaction can be approached from either direction and the terms reactants and products need to be used with caution

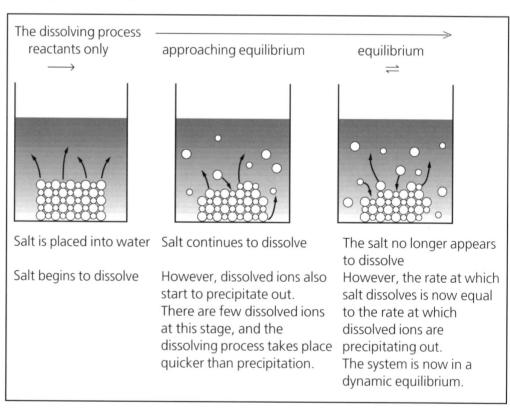

The dissolving process —————————————————————→
reactants only   approaching equilibrium   equilibrium
$\longrightarrow$ $\rightleftharpoons$

Salt is placed into water   Salt continues to dissolve   The salt no longer appears to dissolve

Salt begins to dissolve   However, dissolved ions also   However, the rate at which
                                 start to precipitate out.   salt dissolves is now equal
                                 There are few dissolved ions   to the rate at which
                                 at this stage, and the   dissolved ions are
                                 dissolving process takes place   precipitating out.
                                 quicker than precipitation.   The system is now in a
                                                                   dynamic equilibrium.

Reaching equilibrium

Equilibrium may be approached from either direction

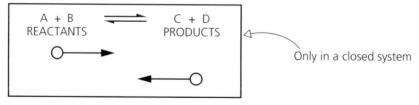

A + B $\rightleftharpoons$ C + D
REACTANTS   PRODUCTS

Only in a closed system

Factors affecting equilibrium

> **Le Chatelier's Principle** states that, if a system in dynamic equilibrium is subjected to a change, processes will occur to minimise this change and to restore equilibrium.

The effect of concentration changes

$N_2(g) + 3H_2(g) \rightleftharpoons 2NH_3(g)$

Change: increase concentration of reactant: $N_2(g)$ or $H_2(g)$

Change opposed: $N_2(g)$ or $H_2(g)$ is removed by forming more $NH_3(g)$

∴ the equilibrium moves to the right (in favour of products).

---

increase concentration of reactant OR reduce concentration of product

$$N_2(g) + 3H_2(g) \rightleftharpoons 2NH_3(g)$$

decrease concentration of reactant OR increase concentration of product

---

The effect of pressure changes

$N_2(g)$	+	$3H_2(g)$	$\rightleftharpoons$	$2NH_3(g)$
1 mol		3 mol		2 mol

4 mol   2 mol

> Gas molecules cause pressure. Reducing the number of gas molecules can decrease pressure.

Change: increase pressure

Change opposed: reducing the number of gas molecules reduces the pressure

∴ 4 mol of gas molecules ⟶ 2 mol of gas molecules

∴ $N_2(g)$ and $H_2(g)$ react to form more $NH_3(g)$

∴ equilibrium moves to the right.

---

more gas molecules (greater gas volume)	pressure increase $\longrightarrow$ $N_2(g) + 3H_2(g) \rightleftharpoons 2NH_3(g)$ $\longleftarrow$ pressure decrease	fewer gas molecules (lower gas volume)

Increasing the pressure also increases the concentration of any gas. This speeds up the reaction but only changes the equilibrium position if
- at least one of the equilibrium species is a gas,
- a change takes place in the number of gas molecules

An exothermic reaction in one direction is endothermic in the opposite direction

The effect of temperature changes

$N_2(g) + 3H_2(g) \rightleftharpoons 2NH_3(g)$ $\Delta H^{\ominus} = -92$ kJ mol^{-1}

Change: decrease temperature

Change opposed: releasing heat energy raises the temperature

∴ equilibrium moves to the right.

---

exothermic process favoured by low temperature

$\Delta H^{\ominus} = +92$ kJ mol^{-1} $N_2(g) + 3H_2(g) \rightleftharpoons 2NH_3(g)$ $\Delta H^{\ominus} = -92$ kJ mol^{-1}

endothermic process favoured by high temperature

The effect of a catalyst

There is **no change** in the equilibrium position. However, the catalyst speeds up both forward and reverse reactions and equilibrium is reached more quickly.

The equilibrium law

The equilibrium constant, K_c

In general, for an equation: $a A + b B \rightleftharpoons c C + d D$,

$$K_c = \frac{[C]_{eq}^c \ [D]_{eq}^d}{[A]_{eq}^a \ [B]_{eq}^b}$$

Working out K_c

For the equilibrium: $H_2(g) + I_2(g) \rightleftharpoons 2HI(g)$,
the equilibrium constant in terms of concentration, K_c, is given by:

$$K_c = \frac{[HI(g)]^2}{[H_2(g)] \ [I_2(g)]}$$

Equilibrium concentrations of $H_2(g)$, $I_2(g)$ and $HI(g)$ are shown below:

$[H_2(g)]$ /mol dm^{-3}	$[I_2(g)]$ /mol dm^{-3}	$[HI(g)]$ /mol dm^{-3}
0.0114	0.0012	0.0252

$$K_c = \frac{[HI(g)]^2}{[H_2(g)] \ [I_2(g)]} = \frac{0.0252^2}{0.0114 \times 0.0012} = 46.4$$

Units of K_c

- In the K_c expression, replace each concentration value by its units:

Substituting units: $K_c = \dfrac{(\text{mol dm}^{-3})^2}{(\text{mol dm}^{-3}) \ (\text{mol dm}^{-3})}$

Units cancel,
$\therefore$ in the equilibrium: $H_2(g) + I_2(g) \rightleftharpoons 2HI(g)$, K_c has no units.

Properties of K_c

- The magnitude of K_c gives an indication of the extent of a chemical reaction:
  $K_c = 1$ indicates an equilibrium halfway between reactants and products
  $K_c = 100$ indicates an equilibrium that is well in favour of the products
  $K_c = 1 \times 10^{-2}$ indicates an equilibrium that is well in favour of the reactants.

- K_c indicates how FAR a reaction proceeds, not how FAST.

- The value of K_c can **only** be changed by altering the temperature.

In an **exothermic** reaction, K_c **decreases** with increasing temperature:
$H_2(g) + I_2(g) \rightleftharpoons 2HI(g)$: $\qquad \Delta H^{\ominus}_{298} = -9.6$ kJ mol^{-1}

temperature/K	K_c
500	160
700	54
1100	25

In an **endothermic** reaction, K_c **increases** with increasing temperature:
$N_2(g) + O_2(g) \rightleftharpoons 2NO(g)$: $\qquad \Delta H^{\ominus}_{298} = +180$ kJ mol^{-1}

temperature/K	K_c
500	5×10^{-13}
700	4×10^{-8}
1100	1×10^{-5}

$[\ ]_{eq}$ means 'equilibrium concentration of . . .'

Use the equation to write K_c

Solid and liquid concentrations are constant – omitted from K_c expressions. K_c expressions contain only species that are gaseous, (g) or aqueous, (aq)

The units must be worked out afresh for each equilibrium

K_c is unaffected by changes in concentration

K_c can ONLY be changed by altering the temperature

(see also pp. 57. – Le Chatelier's Principle)

Working out K_c

0.200 mol CH_3COOH and 0.100 mol C_2H_5OH were mixed together in a total volume of 250 cm³ together with a trace of acid catalyst. The mixture was allowed to reach equilibrium:

$$CH_3COOH + C_2H_5OH \rightleftharpoons CH_3COOC_2H_5 + H_2O$$

Analysis showed that 0.115 mol of CH_3COOH were present at equilibrium.

	CH_3COOH	+	$C_2H_5OH \rightleftharpoons$	$CH_3COOC_2H_5$ +	H_2O
Initial moles	A		B	C	D
Change in moles	$-x$		$-x$	$+x$	$+x$
Equilibrium moles	$A-x$		$B-x$	$C+x$	$D+x$
Equilibrium conc /mol dm⁻³	$\dfrac{A-x}{V}$		$\dfrac{B-x}{V}$	$\dfrac{C+x}{V}$	$\dfrac{D+x}{V}$

V is the total volume of the mixture (250 cm³ in this experiment).

To find K_c

	CH_3COOH	C_2H_5OH	$CH_3COOC_2H_5$	H_2O
no. of moles at start	0.200	0.100	0	0
no. of moles at equilibrium	0.115			

Find the value of 'x', the amount of CH_3COOH that has reacted:

From results for CH_3COOH, $x = 0.200 - 0.115 = 0.085$

The other **changes** are calculated using the reacting quantities of the equation:

	CH_3COOH +	$C_2H_5OH \rightleftharpoons$	$CH_3COOC_2H_5$ +	H_2O
reacting quantities:	1 mol	1 mol	1 mol	1 mol

Then, the **equilibrium** concentration is determined for each component:

	CH_3COOH +	$C_2H_5OH \rightleftharpoons$	$CH_3COOC_2H_5$ +	H_2O
Initial moles	0.200	0.100	0	0
Change in moles	-0.085	-0.085	$+0.085$	$+0.085$
Equilibrium moles	$0.200-0.085$	$0.100-0.085$	$0+0.085$	$0+0.085$
Equilibrium conc /mol dm⁻³	$\dfrac{0.115}{250}$	$\dfrac{0.015}{250}$	$\dfrac{0.085}{250}$	$\dfrac{0.085}{250}$

Write the expression for K_c:

$$K_c = \frac{[CH_3COOC_2H_5]\,[H_2O]}{[CH_3COOH]\,[C_2H_5OH]}$$

Substitute values to calculate K_c:

$$K_c = \frac{\dfrac{0.085}{250} \times \dfrac{0.085}{250}}{\dfrac{0.115}{250} \times \dfrac{0.015}{250}}$$

$\therefore K_c = 4.19$ (No units: all units cancel).

The equilibrium constant, K_p

Equilibria involving gases are usually expressed in terms of K_p, the equilibrium constant in terms of partial pressures.

Partial pressure

In a gas mixture, the *partial pressure* of a gas, p, is:
- the contribution that the gas makes towards the total pressure, P.

Air is a gas mixture with approximate molar proportions of 80% $N_2(g)$ and 20% $O_2(g)$.
- The partial pressure of $N_2(g)$ is 80% of the total pressure.
- The partial pressure of $O_2(g)$ is 20% of the total pressure.

> the mole fraction of a gas A, $x_A = \dfrac{\text{number of moles of A}}{\text{total number of moles in gas mixture}}$
>
> partial pressure of A, p_A = mole fraction of A × total pressure = $x_A \times P$.

The equilibrium constant, K_p

For the equilibrium: $\qquad H_2(g) + I_2(g) \rightleftharpoons 2HI(g)$

> The equilibrium constant in terms of partial pressures, K_p, is given by: $K_p = \dfrac{(p_{HI})^2}{(p_{H_2})\,(p_{I_2})}$

- p means the equilibrium partial pressure.
- Suitable units for partial pressures are Pascals (Pa) or atmospheres (atm); either may be used as long as the same unit is used for all gases.
- The power to which the partial pressures is raised is the *balancing number* in the chemical equation.

Working out K_p

At equilibrium, a reaction mixture contained 1.0 mol $NH_3(g)$, 3.6 mol $H_2(g)$ and 13.5 mol $N_2(g)$. The total equilibrium pressure was 200 kPa. Calculate K_p.

Find the mole fractions and partial pressures:

> Total number of gas moles = 1.0 + 3.6 + 13.5 = 18.1 mol
>
> $\therefore p_{NH_3} = \dfrac{1.0}{18.1} \times 200 = 11$ kPa $\qquad\qquad p_{N_2} = \dfrac{13.5}{18.1} \times 200 = 149$ kPa
>
> $p_{H_2} = \dfrac{3.6}{18.1} \times 200 = 40$ kPa

Calculate K_p:

> For the reaction: $N_2(g) + 3H_2(g) \rightleftharpoons 2NH_3(g)$,
>
> $K_p = \dfrac{(p_{NH_3})^2}{(p_{N_2})\,(p_{H_2})^3} \quad \therefore K_p = \dfrac{(11)^2}{(149)\,(40)^3} = 1.27 \times 10^{-5}$ kPa^{-2}
>
> For units: $K_p = \dfrac{(kPa)^2}{(kPa)\,(kPa)^3} \qquad \therefore$ units of K_p are: kPa^{-2}

Equilibria, rates and industrial processes

Most syllabuses study one or more industrial process, usually including the Haber and Contact processes. You should learn outline details of any process on your syllabus. The principles, however, are common to any similar situation

For many industrial processes, the overall yield of a chemical product can vary considerably, depending on the conditions used.

In deciding which conditions to use, industrial chemists need to consider:
- the availability of the starting materials required for a process
- the equilibrium conditions required to ensure a good yield
- the rate of reaction that should be fast but manageable
- the cost, taking into account energy, cost of materials and of the chemical plant
- the safety of workers from hazardous chemicals, pressures, temperatures, etc.
- any effect on the environment from waste discharges, toxic fumes, etc.

Industrial chemists compare each of these factors to arrive at **compromise** conditions. Although the yield might be **optimised** by using a very high temperature and pressure, this may prove **impractical** for reasons of cost and safety.

The Haber process for the production of NH$_3$

$$N_2(g) + 3H_2(g) \rightleftharpoons 2NH_3(g) \quad \Delta H = -92 \text{ kJ mol}^{-1}$$

The raw materials
- Air, as a source of $N_2(g)$.
- Natural gas, CH_4, and water, H_2O, from which $H_2(g)$ is extracted.

The optimum equilibrium conditions

Optimising the process: these are the ideal conditions to give a maximum yield

Consider Le Chatelier's Principle
- The forward reaction producing NH$_3$ is exothermic, favoured by a **low temperature**.
- The forward reaction produces fewer gas molecules, favoured by a **high pressure**.

The optimum equilibrium conditions for maximum yield are:
- low temperature and high pressure

The need for compromise

Compromising: feasibility, reality and economics are considered

At a low temperature:
- the reaction occurs very slowly because there is insufficient energy to overcome the activation energy of the reaction.

At a high pressure:
- the concentration is high and this will increase the rate
- it is expensive to compress gases
- there are considerable safety implications of a very high pressure: vessel walls need to be very thick to withstand pressure and weaknesses cause danger to workers and potential leakage into the environment.

Compromise conditions

Exam answers need to be sensible and related to relevant issues arising from the process itself.

The compromise conditions used in the Haber Process are such that:
- the temperature is increased sufficiently to allow the reaction to occur at a realistic rate, but not too high to give a minimal yield
- an iron catalyst is used to increase the reaction rate
- a high pressure is used but not too high to be impractical.

The compromise conditions used (200 atm and 450 °C) give a 15% yield only. Any ammonia formed is liquified at −40°C. The unreacted $N_2(g)$ and $H_2(g)$ are recycled.

Brønsted-Lowry theory of acids and bases

Acids

> An acid is a proton, (H^+), donor

Common acids include:
- strong 'mineral' acids H_2SO_4, HCl, HNO_3
- weak acids CH_3COOH, HCOOH, C_6H_5COOH, C_6H_5OH.

Bases

> A base is a proton, (H^+), acceptor

Common bases include:
- metal oxides   MgO, CuO, Na_2O
- metal hydroxides   NaOH, $Mg(OH)_2$, $Fe(OH)_3$
- ammonia and amines NH_3, CH_3NH_2

Alkalis

> An alkali is a base that dissolves in water forming $OH^-(aq)$ ions

There are only a few common alkalis:
- strong alkalis   NaOH(aq), KOH(aq)
- weak alkalis NH_3(aq), $Mg(OH)_2$(aq).

Acid-base equilibria
Acid-base pairs

- Acids and bases co-exist together as conjugate pairs.
- Acid-base pairs are linked by H^+:

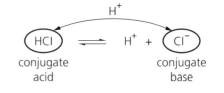

Some conjugate acid-base pairs

	acid				base
hydrochloric acid	HCl	$\rightleftharpoons$	H^+	+	Cl^-
sulphuric acid	H_2SO_4	$\rightleftharpoons$	H^+	+	HSO_4^-
ethanoic acid	CH_3COOH	$\rightleftharpoons$	H^+	+	CH_3COO^-

An acid needs a base
- An acid can only donate a proton if there is a base to accept it!
- Acid-base equilibria contain **two** acid-base *conjugate* pairs.

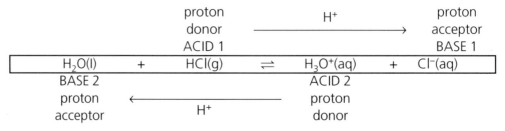

- The 'active' part of an aqueous acid is the *oxonium* ion, H_3O^+ (ACID 2 above).
- It is common practice to simply use H^+(aq) instead of H_3O^+(aq) in equations.

> An acid is a proton donor. A base is a proton acceptor

> A conjugate acid and its conjugate base differ only by H^+: the acid has it, the base doesn't!

> You should be able to identify acid-base pairs in equations such as this

Strength of acids and bases

Different acids donate H^+ to different extents.
The acid-base equilibrium involving an acid, HA, is:
$$HA(aq) + H_2O(l) \rightleftharpoons H_3O^+(aq) + A^-(aq)$$
or more simply:
$$HA(aq) \rightleftharpoons H^+(aq) + A^-(aq)$$

Strong acids

A **strong** acid, e.g nitric acid, is a **good** proton donor:

$$\xrightarrow{\text{equilibrium}}$$

$$HNO_3(aq) \rightleftharpoons H^+(aq) + NO_3^-(aq)$$

- the equilibrium position lies well over to the right
- there is almost **complete dissociation**.

Weak acids

A **weak** acid, e.g ethanoic acid, is a **poor** proton donor:

$$CH_3COOH(aq) \rightleftharpoons H^+(aq) + CH_3COO^-(aq)$$

$$\xleftarrow{\text{equilibrium}}$$

- the equilibrium position lies well over to the left
- there is only partial **dissociation**.

The acid dissociation constant, K_a

The extent to which an acid dissociates is shown by an equilibrium constant called the *acid dissociation constant, K_a*.

For the reaction: $HA(aq) \rightleftharpoons H^+(aq) + A^-(aq)$,

$$K_a = \frac{[H^+(aq)]\ [A^-(aq)]}{[HA(aq)]}$$

units: $K_a = \dfrac{(\text{mol dm}^{-3})^2}{(\text{mol dm}^{-3})}$ units: mol dm^{-3}

- A large value for K_a shows that the extent of dissociation is high - the acid is strong

- A small K_a value shows a small degree of dissociation - the acid is weak

Acid strength and concentration

The distinction between acid strength and concentration is important.

Acid strength:
- is the extent of dissociation of an acid HA into H^+ and A^- in the presence of a proton acceptor such as water
- is measured as K_a in appropriate units determined from the equilibrium equation.

Concentration:
- is the amount of an acid, HA, dissolved in 1 dm^3 of solution. Concentration is measured in mol dm^{-3}.

The pH scale

The pH scale

pH	$[H^+]$ / mol dm^{-3}
0	1
1	1×10^{-1}
2	1×10^{-2}
3	1×10^{-3}
4	1×10^{-4}
5	1×10^{-5}
6	1×10^{-6}
7	1×10^{-7}
8	1×10^{-8}
9	1×10^{-9}
10	1×10^{-10}
11	1×10^{-11}
12	1×10^{-12}
13	1×10^{-13}
14	1×10^{-14}

- The concentrations of $H^+(aq)$ ions in aqueous solutions vary widely between about 10 mol dm^{-3} and about 1×10^{-15} mol dm^{-3}.
- The pH scale is a logarithmic scale used to overcome the problem of using such a large range of these numbers.

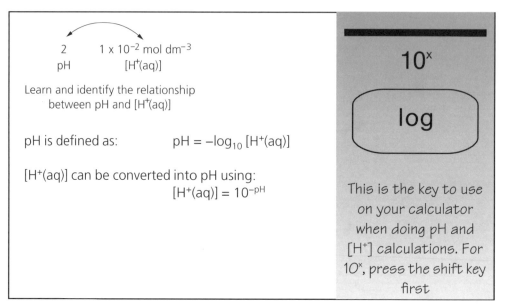

Learn and identify the relationship between pH and $[H^+(aq)]$

pH is defined as: $$pH = -\log_{10}[H^+(aq)]$$

$[H^+(aq)]$ can be converted into pH using: $$[H^+(aq)] = 10^{-pH}$$

10^x

log

This is the key to use on your calculator when doing pH and $[H^+]$ calculations. For 10^x, press the shift key first

What does a pH value mean?
- A **low** value of $[H^+(aq)]$ matches a **high** value of pH.
- A **high** value of $[H^+(aq)]$ matches a **low** value of pH.
- A change of pH of 1 corresponds to a ten-fold change in the $[H^+(aq)]$.
- An acid of pH 4 contains 10 times as many hydrogen ions as an acid of pH 5.

Calculating the pH of strong acids

For a strong acid:
- we can assume complete dissociation
- the concentration of $H^+(aq)$ can be found directly from the acid concentration.

You should be able to convert pH into $[H^+(aq)]$ and *vice versa*.

Example 1
A strong acid, HA, has a concentration of 0.010 mol dm^{-3}. What is the pH?

> Complete dissociation.
> $\therefore [H^+(aq)] = 0.010$ mol dm^{-3}
> $pH = -\log_{10}[H^+(aq)] = -\log_{10}(0.010) = $ **2.0**

Learn this:
$pH = -\log_{10}[H^+]$
and this:
$[H^+] = 10^{-pH}$

Example 2
A strong acid, HA, has a pH of 3.4. What is the concentration of $H^+(aq)$?

> Complete dissociation.
> $\therefore [H^+(aq)] = 10^{-pH} = 10^{-3.4}$ mol dm^{-3}
> $\therefore [H^+(aq)] = $ **3.98×10^{-4}** mol dm^{-3}

Hints for pH calculations

pH calculations are easy once you have learnt to use your calculator. Try the examples above until you can remember the order to press the keys. (Different calculators may need the keys to be pressed in a different order!) Try reversing the process to go back to the original value. Repeat several times until you have this drilled. Now you have learnt to use your calculator, don't borrow another or you will get confused. Finally, look at your answer and decide whether it looks sensible.

Above all, learn how to convert between pH and [H$^+$(aq)] and back again.

Calculating the pH of weak acids

The pH of a weak acid HA can be found from:
- the concentration of the acid
- the value of the acid dissociation constant, K_a.

Assumptions and approximations

Consider the weak acid equilibrium: HA(aq) $\rightleftharpoons$ H$^+$(aq) + A$^-$(aq)
- Assuming that only a very small amount of HA dissociates, the equilibrium concentration of HA(aq) will be very nearly the same as the original concentration.

$$\therefore [HA(aq)]_{equilibrium} \approx [HA(aq)]_{start}$$

- Assuming that there is a negligible concentration of H$^+$ from ionisation of water,

$$[H^+(aq)] \approx [A^-(aq)].$$

Using the approximations

$$K_a = \frac{[H^+(aq)]\ [A^-(aq)]}{[HA(aq)]} \qquad \therefore K_a \approx \frac{[H^+(aq)]^2}{[HA(aq)]}$$

Example

For a weak acid [HA (aq)] = 0.10 mol dm^{-3}, K_a = 1.7 $\times$ 10^{-5} mol dm^{-3} at 25°C. Calculate the pH.

$$K_a = \frac{[H^+(aq)]\ [A^-(aq)]}{[HA(aq)]} \approx \frac{[H^+(aq)]^2}{[HA(aq)]}$$

$$\therefore 1.7 \times 10^{-5} = \frac{[H^+(aq)]^2}{0.10}$$

$$\therefore [H^+(aq)] = \sqrt{0.10 \times 1.7 \times 10^{-5}} = 0.0013 \text{ mol dm}^{-3}$$

pH = $- \log_{10} [H^+(aq)]$

$$\therefore \text{pH} = - \log_{10}(0.0013) = \mathbf{2.9}$$

pK_a

The K_a values are made more manageable if expressed in a logarithmic form, pK_a (see also: [H$^+$(aq)] and pH).

$pK_a = -\log_{10} K_a$
$K_a = 10^{-pKa}$

- A **low** value of K_a matches a **high** value of pK_a.
- A **high** value of K_a matches a **low** value of pK_a.

Comparison of K_a with pK_a

acid		K_a / mol dm^{-3}	pK_a
ethanoic acid	CH$_3$COOH	1.7 $\times$ 10^{-4}	$-\log_{10}(1.7 \times 10^{-4})$ = 3.8
benzoic acid	C$_6$H$_5$COOH	6.3 $\times$ 10^{-5}	$-\log_{10}(6.3 \times 10^{-5})$ = 4.2

Use this approximation in calculations:
$$K_a \approx \frac{[H^+(aq)]^2}{[HA(aq)]}$$

Take care to learn this method. Many marks are dropped on exam papers by students who have not done so!

K_a and pK_a conversions are just like those between pH and H$^+$

The smaller the pK_a value, the stronger the acid

Ionisation of water

The ionisation of water is tiny: just 1 molecule in every 10,000,000

$$\xleftarrow{\text{equilibrium}}$$
$$H_2O(l) \rightleftharpoons H^+(aq) + OH^-(aq)$$

Treating water as a weak acid:
$$K_a = \frac{[H^+(aq)] \ [OH^-(aq)]}{[H_2O(l)]}$$

[$H_2O(l)$] is constant and is included within K_w

Rearranging gives:
$$K_a \times [(H_2O(l)] = [H^+(aq)] [OH^-(aq)]$$
$\underbrace{\qquad\qquad}$
constant

The ionic product of water, K_w, is defined as:
$$K_w = [H^+(aq)] [OH^-(aq)]$$

Hydrogen ion and hydroxide ion concentrations

At 25°C, $[H^+(aq)] \times [OH^-(aq)] = 1 \times 10^{-14}$ mol^2 dm^{-6}

At 25°C, $K_w = 1 \times 10^{-14}$ mol^2 dm^{-6}.

In pure water at 25°C: $[H^+(aq)] = [OH^-(aq)]$

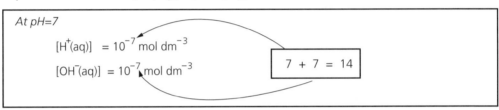

At pH=7
$[H^+(aq)] = 10^{-7}$ mol dm^{-3}
$[OH^-(aq)] = 10^{-7}$ mol dm^{-3}
7 + 7 = 14

In acidic solutions, at 25°C: $[H^+(aq)] > [OH^-(aq)]$

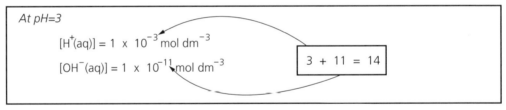

At pH=3
$[H^+(aq)] = 1 \times 10^{-3}$ mol dm^{-3}
$[OH^-(aq)] = 1 \times 10^{-11}$ mol dm^{-3}
3 + 11 = 14

At 25 °C, the negative indices of $[H^+(aq)]$ and $[OH^-(aq)]$ add up to 14

In alkaline solutions, at 25°C: $[OH^-(aq)] > H^+(aq)$

At pH=12
$[H^+(aq)] = 1 \times 10^{-12}$ mol dm^{-3}
$[OH^-(aq)] = 1 \times 10^{-2}$ mol dm^{-3}
12 + 2 = 14

Calculating the pH of strong alkalis

To find the pH of an alkali, first find [H$^+$] using K_w and the [OH$^-$] of the alkali

The pH of a strong alkali can be found using K_w.
- For a strong alkali, we can assume complete dissociation.

Example
A strong alkali, BOH, has a concentration of 0.10 mol dm^{-3}:

$$K_w = [H^+(aq)] [OH^-(aq)] = 1 \times 10^{-14} \text{ mol}^2 \text{ dm}^{-6}$$
$$\therefore [H^+(aq)] = \frac{[OH^-(aq)]}{K_w} = \frac{0.10}{1 \times 10^{-14}} = 1 \times 10^{-13} \text{ mol dm}^{-3}$$
$$pH = -\log_{10}[H^+(aq)] = -\log_{10}(1 \times 10^{-13}) = \mathbf{13}$$

Acid-base indicators

- An acid-base indicator is a weak acid.
- An indicator, HIn, and its conjugate base, In⁻, have different colours, e.g. for methyl orange:

$$HIn(aq) \rightleftharpoons H^+(aq) + In^-(aq)$$
$$\textit{red} \qquad\qquad \textit{yellow}$$

This idea is very similar to that explaining the action of buffer solutions pp. 69

Addition of an acid, H⁺

- The concentration of H⁺ in the equilibrium is increased.
- The pH change is opposed and the equilibrium moves to the left, removing most of the [H⁺(aq)] and forming HIn(aq).
- The methyl orange turns red.

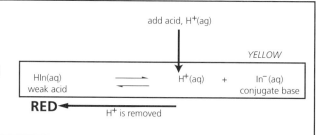

Addition of an alkali, OH⁻

- The added OH⁻ reacts with the small amount of H⁺ present at equilibrium:
  $$H^+(aq) + OH^-(aq) \longrightarrow H_2O(l)$$
- The pH change is opposed and the equilibrium moves to the right, restoring most of the [H⁺(aq)].
- The methyl orange turns yellow.

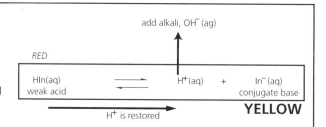

Indicators and end-points

Each indicator has its own end-point pH at which its colour changes. This is called the pK$_{in}$ of the indicator

At the end-point of a titration using methyl orange as indicator:
- HIn and In⁻ are present in equal concentrations
- the colour is orange, midway between the acid colour (red) and the alkali colour (yellow)
- the pH of the end-point is called the pK_{in} value of the indicator.

pH ranges for common indicators

- An indicator changes colour over a range of about 2 pH units within which is the pK_{in} value of the indicator.

pH	0	1	2	3	4	5	6	7	8	9	10	11	12	13	14
			RED ⟷ YELLOW methyl orange, pK_{in} = 3.7												
						YELLOW ⟷ BLUE bromothymol blue, pK_{in} = 7.0									
							COLOURLESS ⟷ PINK phenolphthalein, pK_{in} = 9.3								

Choosing an indicator using titration curves

Referring to each of the titration curves below.

- Note the sharp change in pH at the *end-point* or *equivalence point* of the titration.
- The sharp change in pH is brought about by a very small addition of acid or alkali, i.e. for the addition of one drop.
- The indicator is only suitable if its pK_{in} value is within the pH range of the near vertical portion of the titration curve.
- On the titration curves, the pK_{in} values are shown for phenolphthalein (*P*), bromothymol blue (*BB*) and methyl orange (*MO*).

Bromothymol blue might seem to be the ideal indicator with its pK_{in} value of 7.0.
However, its colour change is difficult to see and both methyl orange and phenolphthalein give colour changes that are much easier to determine

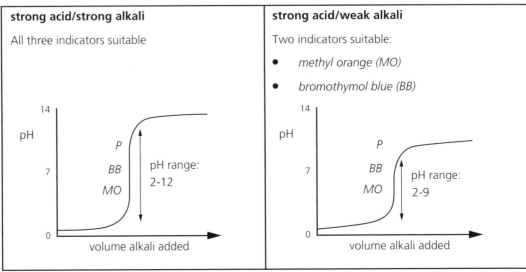

strong acid/strong alkali

All three indicators suitable

pH range: 2-12

strong acid/weak alkali

Two indicators suitable:

- *methyl orange (MO)*
- *bromothymol blue (BB)*

pH range: 2-9

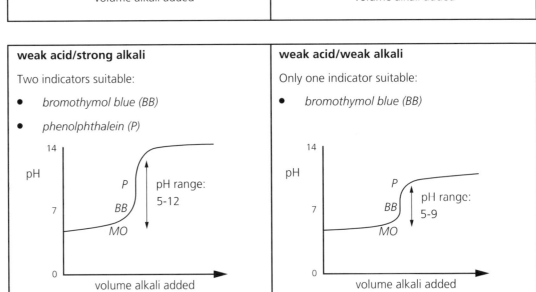

weak acid/strong alkali

Two indicators suitable:

- *bromothymol blue (BB)*
- *phenolphthalein (P)*

pH range: 5-12

weak acid/weak alkali

Only one indicator suitable:

- *bromothymol blue (BB)*

pH range: 5-9

Titrations of weak acid/weak alkalis

It is very difficult to see a sharp colour change for titrations involving a weak acid and a weak alkali. In such cases, the pH is often followed using a pH meter.

Buffer solutions

- A buffer solution 'resists' pH changes.
- Despite the addition of an acid or an alkali, a buffer solution maintains a near constant pH, effectively removing most of any added acid or alkali.
- A buffer solution is a mixture of a weak acid, HA, and its conjugate base, A⁻:

$$HA(aq) \rightleftharpoons H^+(aq) + A^-(aq)$$
weak acid   *conjugate base*

- The concentration of $H^+(aq)$ ions is very small compared with $HA(aq)$ or $A^-(aq)$.

Addition of an acid, H^+

- The concentration of H^+ in the equilibrium is increased.
- The pH change is opposed and the equilibrium moves to the left, removing most of the $[H^+(aq)]$.
- The **conjugate base A⁻ removes [H⁺]**

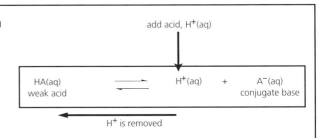

Addition of an alkali, OH^-

- The added OH^- reacts with the small amount of H^+ present at equilibrium:
  $H^+(aq) + OH^-(aq) \longrightarrow H_2O(l)$
- The pH change is opposed and the equilibrium moves to the right, replacing most of the $[H^+(aq)]$.
- The **weak acid HA replaces [H⁺]**.

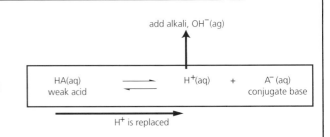

Common buffer solutions

An acidic buffer
- Ethanoic acid as the weak acid, CH_3COOH.
- Sodium ethanoate, $CH_3COO^-Na^+$, as a source of the conjugate base, CH_3COO^-.

An alkaline buffer
- Ammonium chloride, $NH_4^+Cl^-$, as a source of the weak acid, NH_4^+.
- Ammonia as the conjugate base, NH_3.

Calculations involving buffer solutions

The pH of a buffer solution depends upon:
- the ratio of the weak acid and conjugate base
- the acid dissociation constant, K_a, for the buffer system.

For a buffer solution containing the weak acid, HA, and its conjugate base, A⁻,

$$K_a = \frac{[H^+(aq)]\ [A^-(aq)]}{[HA(aq)]} \qquad \therefore [H^+(aq)] = K_a \times \frac{[HA(aq)]}{[A^-(aq)]}$$

Example
Calculate the pH of a buffer solution containing 0.30 mol dm⁻³ of $CH_3COOH(aq)$ and 0.10 mol dm⁻³ $CH_3COO^-(aq)$. [K_a of $CH_3COOH = 1.7 \times 10^{-5}$ mol dm⁻³]

$$[H^+(aq)] = K_a \times \frac{[HA(aq)]}{[A^-(aq)]} \qquad \therefore [H^+(aq)] = 1.7 \times 10^{-5} \times \frac{0.30}{0.10}$$
$$= 5.1 \times 10^{-5} \text{ mol dm}^{-3}$$
$$\therefore pH = -\log_{10}[H^+(aq)] = -\log_{10}(5.1 \times 10^{-5}) \qquad \therefore \text{pH of the buffer} = \textbf{4.3}$$

7 Rates

Reaction rates

The rate of a reaction is usually measured as the change in concentration of a reaction species with time.

For a reaction: **A** $\longrightarrow$ **B**, the reaction rate is:
- the rate of decrease in concentration of **A** or
- the rate of increase in concentration of **B**.

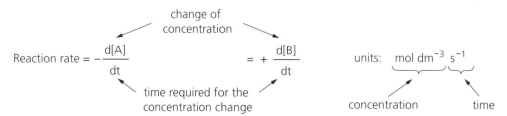

A reaction rate is expressed as a positive value. For the reactant A, the negative sign shows a decreasing concentration with time. For the product B, the positive sign shows increasing concentration

Factors which affect a reaction rate

A temperature change
- A small temperature change can have a dramatic effect on reaction rate. Many reactions double their rate for a 10°C rise in temperature.

A concentration change
- More concentrated chemicals usually react quicker.

The surface area of solid reactants
- More surface for reaction (powder versus solid) allows more contact between the available reactants, increasing the rate.

The presence of a catalyst
- Each catalyst speeds up only some reactions.

The presence of light
- Radiation is required for some reactions, such as photosynthesis, to occur. Often the frequency of the light is important.

For activation energy, see also Chemical energetics pp. 49

Collision theory

Collisions can occur between particles in constant random motion:
- molecules in gases
- any species in solution.

A reaction can occur between these particles only if:
- a collision takes place
- the collision has sufficient energy to overcome the *activation energy* of the reaction.

Only those collisions of sufficient energy to overcome the activation energy lead to a reaction

Changing the rate of reaction

The rate of a reaction can increase if there are **more frequent collisions** achieved by:

increased concentration:
- more particles, so there will be more collisions every second

increased temperature:
- molecules move faster causing more collisions each second
- the increased speed of the molecules results in collisions that are more energetic.

The Boltzmann distribution

The Boltzmann distribution shows the distribution of molecular energies in a gas at constant temperature.

Characteristics of the Boltzmann distribution
- Most gas molecules have energies within a comparatively narrow range.
- No molecules have an energy of zero.
- The curve will only meet the energy axis at an energy of infinity.
- The total number of gas molecules is the area under the distribution curve.

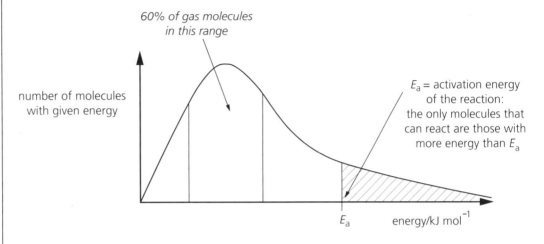

The Boltzmann distribution curves and temperature
temperature, T_2 > temperature, T_1

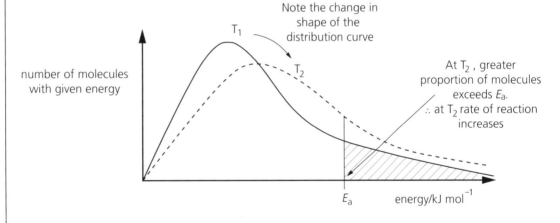

Increasing the temperature moves the distribution curve

An increase in temperature increases the rate of a reaction because:
- more molecules exceed the activation energy
- the molecules are now moving faster overall, producing more frequent collisions
- the Boltzmann distribution curve is displaced to the right with the peak lower
- average energy is now increased.

The total area is the same under each distribution curve:
- only the temperature has changed
- the number of molecules is the same.

Increasing the temperature does not change the activation energy: more molecules now exceed the activation energy

Catalysts

A catalyst alters the rate of a chemical reaction, but is unchanged at the end of the reaction.

Catalysts and energy

A catalyst achieves a faster rate for the reaction by providing an alternative route with lower activation energy.

- Activation energy without catalyst, E_a > activation energy with catalyst, E_c

Energy pathway diagram

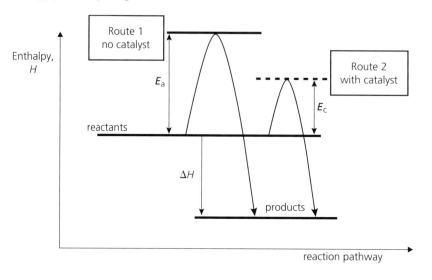

Boltzmann distribution curve with and without a catalyst

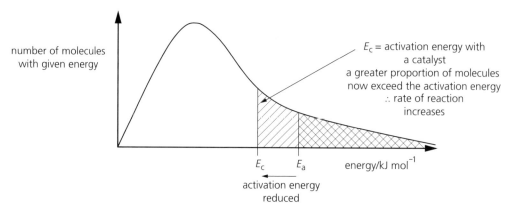

A catalyst increases the rate of a reaction because:

- the reaction proceeds by a different route
- there is now a new and lower activation energy, E_c
- more molecules exceed the lower activation energy.

Heterogeneous catalysis

The catalyst is in different phase from the reactants.

How do they work?
Examples:

Haber Process for ammonia

$N_2(g) + 3H_2(g) \rightleftharpoons 2NH_3(g)$

- The equilibrium process is catalysed by an iron catalyst, $Fe(s)$.
- Reactants are gaseous, the catalyst is a solid.

> The key to this process is adsorption of reactants on the surface of the catalyst

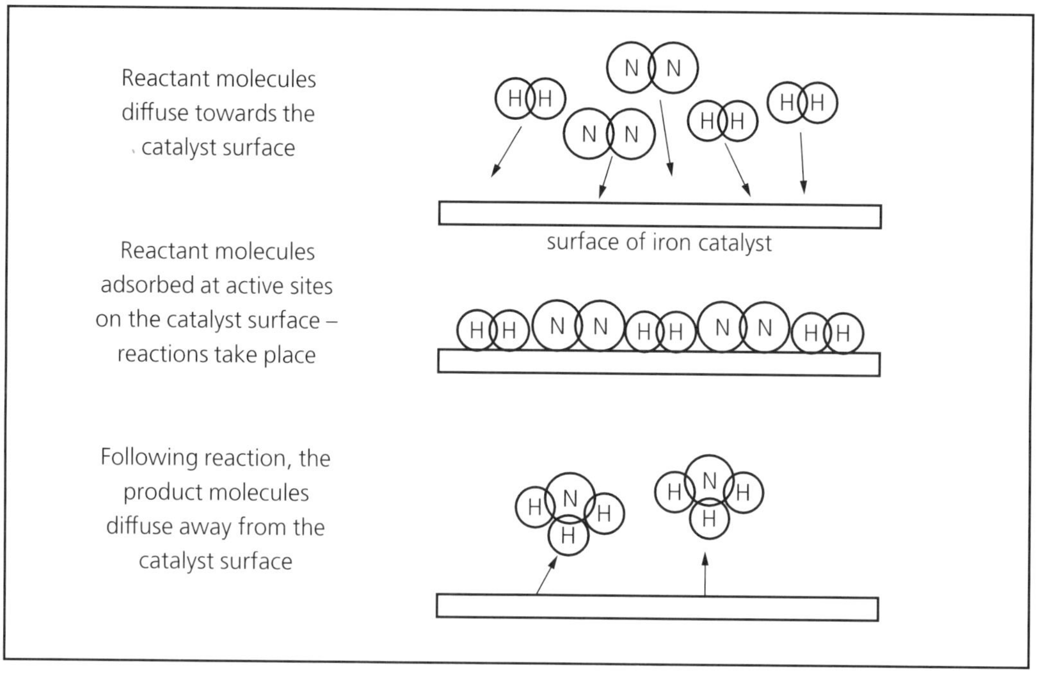

Reactant molecules diffuse towards the catalyst surface

surface of iron catalyst

Reactant molecules adsorbed at active sites on the catalyst surface – reactions take place

Following reaction, the product molecules diffuse away from the catalyst surface

Contact Process for sulphur trioxide (and subsequently sulphuric acid)

$2SO_2(g) + O_2(g) \rightleftharpoons 2SO_3(g)$
- The equilibrium process is catalysed by vanadium(V) oxide, $V_2O_5(s)$.
- Reactants are gaseous, the catalyst is a solid.

> Many heterogeneous catalysts are transition metals or their compounds

Catalytic converters

A catalytic converter in a car's exhaust system uses a Rh/Pt/Pd catalyst impregnated on a ceramic honeycomb with a large surface area.

CO and NO are produced in a car engine.
- CO: formed from incomplete combustion of hydrocarbons
- NO: formed from reaction of N_2 and O_2 in engine/at high temperature.

These gases temporarily bond to the catalyst's surface and it is here that reaction takes place. The products then leave the surface, allowing for further reaction on the catalyst's surface. The catalytic converter removes much of this pollution in a series of reactions. e.g.

$2CO(g) + 2NO(g) \longrightarrow 2CO_2(g) + N_2(g)$

Unleaded petrol is essential or lead will 'poison' the catalyst:
- the catalyst becomes coated with a thin film of lead
- the lead prevents the polluting gases from reaching and interacting with the catalyst.

Homogeneous catalysis

The catalyst is in the same phase as the reactants.

How do they work?
- A reaction involving a catalyst proceeds via an intermediate state.
- Subsequently, the catalyst is regenerated, allowing further reaction.

Examples:

Ester hydrolysis, catalysed by aqueous acid

In the hydrolysis of an ester, reactants and catalyst are all aqueous:

$$\text{H}^+\text{(aq) catalyst}$$
$$CH_3COOC_2H_5(aq) + H_2O(l) \rightleftharpoons CH_3COOH(aq) + C_2H_5OH(aq)$$

- The H^+ (aq) catalyst speeds up the forward and reverse reactions.
- The equilibrium position is established quicker.

The breakdown of atmospheric ozone, catalysed by •Cl radicals

•Cl free radicals are recycled in a chain reaction.

chain reaction: $O_3(g) + \bullet Cl(g) \longrightarrow O_2(g) + \bullet ClO(g)$
$\ O_3(g) + \bullet ClO(g) \longrightarrow 2O_2(g) + \bullet Cl(g)$
overall: $2O_3(g) \longrightarrow 3O_2(g)$

The reaction between I⁻ and $S_2O_8^{2-}$, catalysed by aqueous Fe^{2+} ions

- The reaction between I^- and $S_2O_8^{2-}$ is very slow.
- This reaction is catalysed by Fe^{2+} ions.
- Fe^{2+} ions are recycled in a chain reaction.

chain reaction: $S_2O_8^{2-}(aq) + 2Fe^{2+}(aq) \longrightarrow 2SO_4^{2-}(aq) + 2Fe^{3+}(aq)$
$\ 2Fe^{3+}(aq) + 2I^-(aq) \longrightarrow I_2(aq) + 2Fe^{2+}(aq)$
overall: $2I^-(aq) + S_2O_8^{2-}(aq) \longrightarrow I_2(aq) + 2SO_4^{2-}(aq)$

Enzymes

- Biological catalysts, now being used as immobilised enzymes in industry.
- Work by a lock-and-key mechanism.
- E.g. zymase in yeast (used in brewing); the production of high-fructose syrup.

Advantages include
- Highly specific reaction.
- Reactions often take place at much lower temperatures than conventional catalysts.

Immobilised enzymes
- Can be used in a continuous process.
- Are less easily denatured than conventional enzyme use.
- Are easily recycled for future use.

You do not need to remember details of these examples

So a •Cl catalyst is used up, but it is then regenerated to be used again in a chain reaction – the middleman of chemistry

During catalysis, transition metal ions change their oxidation states and bond via d-orbitals

Simple rate equations; orders of reaction; rate constants

The Rate Law

The Rate Law is the experimentally determined relationship showing how the rate of a reaction is affected by the concentrations of reactants.

For an equation: A + B $\longrightarrow$ C:

- the experimentally determined rate = $k[A]^m[B]^n$
- m and n are the orders of reaction with respect to A and B respectively
- the overall order of reaction is m+n
- k is the rate constant
- the reaction rate is measured as the change in concentration of a reaction species with time in mol dm^{-3} s^{-1}.

Working out the rate constant, k

Example

For an equation: A + B $\longrightarrow$ C
it was found experimentally that:

$$Rate = k\,[A]^1\,[B]^2$$

The order is 1 (first order) with respect to A	The order is 2 (second order) with respect to B

• If [B] is kept constant and
   [A] × 2,   rate doubles;
   [A] × 4,   rate quadruples.
	• If [A] is kept constant and
	   [B] × 2, rate quadruples;
	   [B] × 4, rate × 16.

The overall order of this reaction = (order of A) + (order of B) = 1+2 = 3

Reactants with zero order

If the order is 0 (zero order) with respect to a reactant:

- the rate is unaffected by changes in concentration of that reactant (any number to the power zero = 1).

Example

In the reaction, P + Q $\longrightarrow$ R:

- the experimentally determined order with respect to P is 2
- the experimentally determined order with respect to Q is 0.

> Rate = $k\,[P]^2\,[Q]^0$
> Because $[Q]^0 = 1$, this term is usually omitted:
> $\therefore$ Rate = $k\,[P]^2$

How can a rate equation be determined experimentally?

Initial rates method

The initial rate

For a reaction, X + Y $\longrightarrow$ Z, a series of experiments is carried out using different **initial** concentrations of X and Y.

For each experiment:

- plot a concentration/time graph and
- measure the initial rate from the graph as the tangent drawn at time =0.

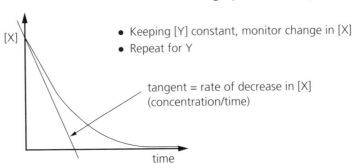

- Keeping [Y] constant, monitor change in [X]
- Repeat for Y

tangent = rate of decrease in [X]
(concentration/time)

The rate of the reaction is measured from the tangent of a concentration /time graph

Note that although the gradient of the graph above is negative (showing a decrease in the concentration of X), the reaction rate is positive, given by:

$$\text{Reaction rate} = -\frac{d[X]}{dt}$$

The negative sign in this rate expression converts a negative concentration change into a positive reaction rate

Results

Experiment	[X(aq)] / mol dm^{-3}	[Y(aq)] / mol dm^{-3}	Initial rate / mol dm^{-3}s^{-1}
1	1.0×10^{-2}	1.0×10^{-2}	0.5×10^{-3}
2	2.0×10^{-2}	1.0×10^{-2}	2.0×10^{-3}
3	2.0×10^{-2}	2.0×10^{-2}	4.0×10^{-3}

To find the orders and the rate equation for this reaction

> *Using experiments 1 and 2:*
> [Y(aq)] constant
> [X(aq)] doubled, rate × 4   ∴ Order with respect to X(aq) = 2
> *Using experiments 2 and 3:*
> [X(aq)] constant
> [Y(aq)] doubled, rate doubles: ∴ Order with respect to Y(aq) = 1
> *The Rate Equation is:*
> Rate = k [X]^2 [Y]

To find the rate constant, k, for this reaction

You will get the same value of k from the results of any of the experimental runs

> *Rearrange the rate equation:*
> The rate constant, $k = \dfrac{\text{Rate}}{[X]^2\ [Y]}$
>
> *Calculate k using values from Experiment 2:*
> $k = \dfrac{(2.0 \times 10^{-3})}{(2.0 \times 10^{-2})^2\ (1.0 \times 10^{-2})} = 500\ \text{dm}^6\ \text{mol}^{-2}\ \text{s}^{-1}$
>
> *Units are found by substituting each concentration term by its units:*
> Units of $k = \dfrac{(\text{mol dm}^{-3}\text{s}^{-1})}{(\text{mol dm}^{-3})^2\ (\text{mol dm}^{-3})} = \text{dm}^6\ \text{mol}^{-2}\ \text{s}^{-1}$

The units depend upon each rate equation

Shapes of graphs

Concentration/time graphs

- Experimental results usually enable the concentration of a reactant or product to be measured at various times during the reaction.
- A concentration/time graph can be plotted from these experimental results.
- The shape of this graph indicates the order of the reaction.

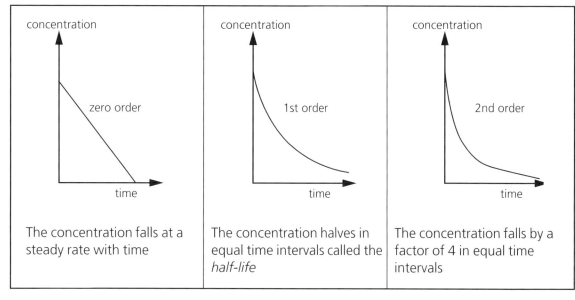

The concentration falls at a steady rate with time	The concentration halves in equal time intervals called the *half-life*	The concentration falls by a factor of 4 in equal time intervals

The half-life curve of a 1st order reaction is concentration independent

Rate/concentration graphs

- A concentration/time graph is first plotted.
- The gradient of the concentration/time graph is a measure of the rate of a reaction.
- Tangents are drawn at several time values on a concentration/time graph giving values of reaction rates.
- A second graph can then be plotted of rate against concentration.
- The shape of this graph confirms the order of the reaction.

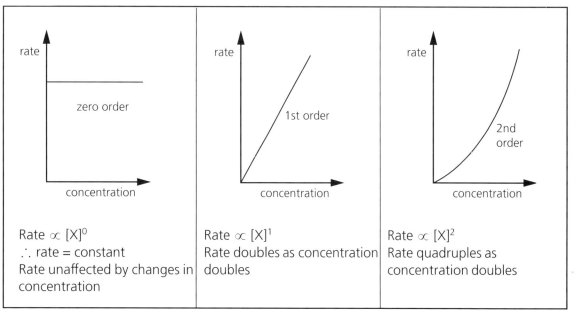

Rate $\propto [X]^0$ ∴ rate = constant Rate unaffected by changes in concentration	Rate $\propto [X]^1$ Rate doubles as concentration doubles	Rate $\propto [X]^2$ Rate quadruples as concentration doubles

For a 2nd order relationship, a graph of rate against log[X] gives a straight line

Rate equations and reaction mechanisms

A balanced equation represents the overall reaction.
It does not reveal the mechanism that achieves it.
Evidence for the mechanism comes from the rate equation

- A reaction mechanism is the route by which a reaction is achieved.
- The rate equation of a reaction can provide information about this mechanism by identifying the *slowest* stage of a reaction sequence.

Example. The hydrolysis of halogenoalkanes

Primary halogenoalkanes
The primary halogenoalkane, CH_3Br, is hydrolysed by aqueous alkali:
$$CH_3Br + OH^- \longrightarrow CH_3OH + Br^-$$
Experiments show that the rate equation is:
$$Rate = k[CH_3Br][OH^-]$$
This rate equation shows that:
- the rate is determined by a reaction step involving **both** CH_3Br *and* OH^-.

This supports the one-stage mechanism:
$$CH_3Br + OH^- \longrightarrow CH_3OH + Br^-$$

$$Rate = k[CH_3Br][OH^-]$$

For more details of these mechanisms, see 'Halogeno-alkanes' pp. 98

Tertiary halogenoalkanes
The tertiary halogenoalkane, $(CH_3)_3CBr$, is hydrolysed by aqueous alkali:
$$(CH_3)_3CBr + OH^- \longrightarrow (CH_3)_3COH + Br^-$$

Experiments show that the rate equation is:
$$Rate = k[(CH_3)_3CBr]$$
This rate equation shows that:
- the rate is determined solely by the concentration of $(CH_3)_3CBr$
- the concentration of OH^- has no effect on the rate.

*A possible stage in the reaction mechanism including **just** $(CH_3)_3CBr$ is:*
$$(CH_3)_3CBr \longrightarrow (CH_3)_3C^+ + Br^-$$

You are not expected to remember these examples.
You are expected to interpret data, to identify a rate-determining step and to suggest a reaction mechanism

$$Rate = k[(CH_3)_3CBr]$$

This supports the two-stage mechanism:

step 1 $(CH_3)_3CBr \longrightarrow (CH_3)_3C^+ + Br^-$ **SLOW**   **rate-determining step**
step 2 $(CH_3)_3C^+ + OH^- \longrightarrow (CH_3)_3COH$ **FAST**

- The rate of the reaction is controlled mainly by the slowest step.
- The slowest step of a mechanism is called the **rate-determining step**.
- The orders in the rate equation match the number of molecules involved in the rate-determining step - in this case, 1 molecule of $(CH_3)_3CBr$.

In this reaction:

- step 1 is **unimolecular** (involves one molecule) - it has a **molecularity** of 1
- step 2 is **bimolecular** (involves two molecules) - it has a **molecularity** of 2.

8 Electrode potentials

Redox reactions

Oxidation and reduction

OIL
RIG

↓

Oxidation
Is
Loss
Reduction
Is
Gain

- Oxidation and reduction take place together in a *redox* reaction.
- A redox reaction involves transfer of electrons.

Something is **oxidised** if:	Something is **reduced** if:
• it gains oxygen • it loses electrons	• it loses oxygen • it gains electrons

The reaction of magnesium and chlorine:

reaction	$Mg + Cl_2 \longrightarrow MgCl_2$	
electron transfer	$Mg \longrightarrow Mg^{2+} + 2e^-$	oxidation (loss of electrons)
	$Cl_2 + 2e^- \longrightarrow 2Cl^-$	reduction (gain of electrons)

Oxidation state

Oxidation numbers are useful for identifying redox reactions in which electron loss and electron gain are not easy to see

Oxidation states or oxidation numbers provide a means of accounting for electrons.

Principal rules

1. Any uncombined element has an oxidation number of zero: C, zero; O_2, zero.
2. An ion of an element has an oxidation number equal to its charge:
   Na^+, +1; Mg^{2+}, +2; Cl^-, −1.
3. Combined oxygen usually has an oxidation number of −2.
4. Combined hydrogen usually has an oxidation number of +1.
5. In a compound, the total of all of the oxidation numbers is zero:
   NaCl, +1, −1; CO_2, +4, (−2) × 2 gives a total of zero.
6. In a molecular ion, the total of all oxidation numbers is equal to the overall charge on the ion: NO_3^-, +5, (−2) × 3 gives a total charge of −1.
7. Combined fluorine always has an oxidation number of −1.

Oxidation number applies to each atom in a species

Main exceptions
1. In compounds with fluorine and in peroxides, the oxidation number of oxygen is not −2 and must be calculated from other oxidation numbers.
2. In metal hydrides, the oxidation number of hydrogen is −1.

Equations and oxidation number

Oxidation is an increase in oxidation number. Reduction is a decrease in oxidation number

	$Cr_2O_3(s)$	+	$2Al(s)$	$\longrightarrow$	$Al_2O_3(s)$	+	$2Cr(s)$
oxidation	+3 −2		0		+3 −2		0
numbers	+3 −2		0		+3 −2		0
	−2				−2		
	0				0		

The oxidation number changes in the above reaction are:

Cr:	$+3 \longrightarrow 0$	reduction	oxidation number decreases
Al:	$0 \longrightarrow +3$	oxidation	oxidation number increases

Oxidising and reducing agents

Oxidising agent
A reactant that **removes** electrons from another, e.g. F_2, Cl_2, O_2

Reducing agent
A reactant that **gives** electrons to another, e.g. Na, Fe, Zn

Half-equations
Used to show the fate of an oxidised or reduced species.
- Ensure that the number of electrons makes the net charge the same on each side of the half-equation:

	Fe^{3+}	+	e^-	$\rightleftharpoons$	Fe^{2+}
charge:	+3		−1		+2
net charge is the same:		+2			+2

- The oxidised form Fe^{3+} is the oxidising agent.
- The reduced form Fe^{2+} is the reducing agent.
- The reversible sign shows that the reaction can proceed in either direction.

Electrochemical cells

Half-cells using metals and their metal ions

Example: A zinc-copper cell
Zinc reacts with aqueous copper(II) ions in a redox reaction:
$$Zn(s) + Cu^{2+}(aq) \longrightarrow Zn^{2+}(aq) + Cu(s)$$
oxidation: $Zn(s) \longrightarrow Zn^{2+}(aq) + 2e^-$
reduction: $Cu^{2+}(aq) + 2e^- \longrightarrow Cu(s)$

In an electrochemical cell:
- the oxidation and reduction processes take place separately
- electrons travel along a connecting wire between two half-cells
- the circuit is completed using a *salt bridge* which transfers ions between the half-cells.

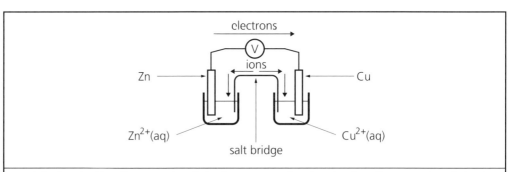

oxidation half-cell: Zn and Zn^{2+}(aq)
- Zn is oxidised to Zn^{2+}:
  $Zn(s) \longrightarrow Zn^{2+}(aq) + 2e^-$
- electrons are supplied to the external circuit
- the polarity is negative.

reduction half-cell: Cu and Cu^{2+}(aq)
- Cu^{2+} is reduced to Cu:
  $Cu^{2+}(aq) + 2e^- \longrightarrow Cu(s)$
- electrons are taken from the external circuit
- the polarity is positive.

The measured cell e.m.f. of 1.10 V indicates that there is a potential difference of 1.10 V between the copper and zinc half-cells.

Half-cells using ions of different oxidation states

For aqueous ions of different oxidation states, an inert electrode of platinum is used to allow electrons to be conducted into and out of the solution.

Example: A half-cell using $Fe^{3+}(aq)/Fe^{2+}(aq)$

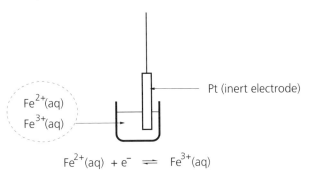

$$Fe^{2+}(aq) + e^- \rightleftharpoons Fe^{3+}(aq)$$

Standard electrode potentials

A hydrogen half-cell is used as the standard for the measurement of standard electrode potentials.

> The standard electrode potential of a half-cell is the e.m.f. of a half-cell compared with a standard hydrogen half-cell.
> All measurements are at 298 K with solution concentrations of 1 mol dm^{-3} and gas pressures of 100 kPa (1 atmosphere).

Solutions in a standard cell have a concentration of 1 mol dm^{-3}

Measuring a standard electrode potential

A high-resistance voltmeter is used to minimise the current that flows

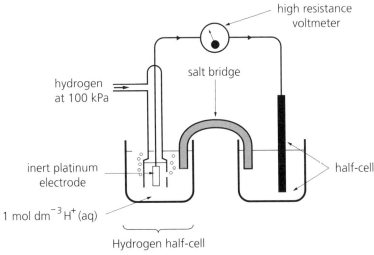

- The hydrogen half-cell typically contains 1 mol dm^{-3} hydrochloric acid as the source of H$^+$(aq).
- The standard electrode potential of a half-cell represents its contribution to the cell e.m.f. .
- The sign of the standard electrode potential of a half-cell indicates its polarity compared with the hydrogen half-cell.
- The contribution made by the hydrogen half-cell to the cell e.m.f. is defined as 0.0 V.

Calculating a standard cell potential from $E^\ominus$ values

The electrochemical series

Standard electrode potentials can be listed as an electrochemical series:

	electrode reaction					$E^\ominus$/V	
strongest	$F_2(g)$	+	$2e^-$	$\rightleftharpoons$	$2F^-(aq)$	+2.87	
oxidising	$Cl_2(g)$	+	$2e^-$	$\rightleftharpoons$	$2Cl^-(aq)$	+1.36	
agent	$Br_2(g)$	+	$2e^-$	$\rightleftharpoons$	$2Br^-(aq)$	+1.07	
	$Ag^+(aq)$	+	e^-	$\rightleftharpoons$	$Ag(s)$	+0.80	
	$Cu^{2+}(aq)$	+	$2e^-$	$\rightleftharpoons$	$Cu(s)$	+0.34	
	$2H^+(aq)$	+	$2e^-$	$\rightleftharpoons$	$H_2(g)$	0	
	$Fe^{2+}(aq)$	+	$2e^-$	$\rightleftharpoons$	$Fe(s)$	−0.44	*strongest*
	$Zn^{2+}(aq)$	+	$2e^-$	$\rightleftharpoons$	$Zn(s)$	−0.76	*reducing*
	$K^+(aq)$	+	e^-	$\rightleftharpoons$	$K(s)$	−2.92	*agent*

Some books show the electrochemical series in the opposite order: from negative to positive

Calculating a standard cell potential

Identify the two relevant half-reactions and the polarity of each electrode.

> The more positive of the two systems is the positive terminal of the cell.
> $Cu^{2+}(aq)$ + $2e^-$ $\rightleftharpoons$ $Cu(s)$ $E^\ominus = +0.34\,V$ *positive terminal*
> $Fe^{2+}(aq)$ + $2e^-$ $\rightleftharpoons$ $Fe(s)$ $E^\ominus = -0.44\,V$ *negative terminal*

$E^\ominus_{cell}$ is the difference between the standard electrode potentials

The standard electrode potential is the difference between the $E^\ominus$ values:

> Subtract the $E^\ominus$ of the negative terminal from the $E^\ominus$ of the positive terminal:
> $E^\ominus_{cell} = E^\ominus_{+terminal} - E^\ominus_{-terminal}$
> $\therefore E^\ominus_{cell} = (+0.34) - (-0.44) = +0.78\,V$

Work out the actual direction of the half equations

The more negative half-equation is reversed

> Reverse the more negative half-reaction to give each half-cell reaction:
> $Cu^{2+}(aq) + 2e^- \rightarrow Cu(s)$ *reaction at positive terminal*
> $Fe(s) \rightarrow Fe^{2+}(aq) + 2e^-$ *reaction at negative terminal*

The overall cell reaction can be found by adding the half-equations. If necessary, first balance the electrons.

> $Cu^{2+}(aq)$ + $Fe(s)$ $\longrightarrow$ $Cu(s)$ + $Fe^{2+}(aq)$

Electrode potentials and the concentration of the aqueous ion

- Non-standard conditions alter the value of an electrode potential.
- A concentration of less then 1 mol dm^{-3} gives a more negative electrode potential:

$Cu^{2+}(aq) + 2e^- \rightleftharpoons Cu(s)$

By Le Chatelier's Principle,

> *change:* reduce the concentration of $Cu^{2+}(aq)$:
> - equilibrium adjusts to oppose change moving equilibrium to the left
> - more electrons produced: electrode potential more negative.

In general:
- decreasing concentration gives a more negative electrode potential.
- increasing concentration gives a more positive electrode potential.

Predicting redox reactions using standard cell potentials

The direction of any aqueous redox reaction can be predicted provided that the standard electrode potentials of the relevant half-reactions are known.

First, identify the two relevant half-equations.
- The more negative of the two systems supplies the electrons.

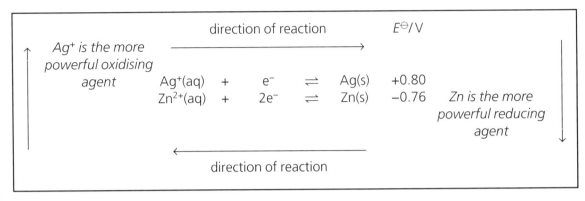

To write an overall equation:
- reverse the more negative half-equation to give the actual half-equations:
$$Ag^+(aq) + e^- \longrightarrow Ag(s)$$
$$Zn(s) \longrightarrow Zn^{2+}(aq) + 2e^-$$

Zn reaction reversed →

- The number of electrons is made the same in both equations:
$$2Ag^+(aq) + 2e^- \longrightarrow 2Ag(s)$$
$$Zn(s) \longrightarrow Zn^{2+}(aq) + 2e^-$$

Ag^+ reaction ×2 →

- The equations are then added:
$$2Ag^+(aq) + 2e^- + Zn(s) \longrightarrow 2Ag(s) + Zn^{2+}(aq) + 2e^-$$

- Any species appearing on both sides are cancelled
$$2Ag^+(aq) + Zn(s) \longrightarrow 2Ag(s) + Zn^{2+}(aq)$$

Cancel electrons to → give the overall equation

- Finally, check that the net charge balances on each side of the equation:

$$2Ag^+(aq) + Zn(s) \longrightarrow 2Ag(s) + Zn^{2+}(aq)$$
charge: $2 \times (+1)$ 0 0 $+2$

net charge is the same: $+2$ $+2$

Will a reaction take place?

> Remember that these are equilibrium processes. Predictions can be made but these give no indication of the reaction rate which may be extremely slow, caused by a large activation energy.
> The actual conditions used may also be different from the standard conditions used to record $E^{\ominus}$ values.

- The larger the difference between $E^{\ominus}$ values, the more likely that a reaction will take place.
- If the difference between $E^{\ominus}$ values is less than 0.4 V, then a reaction is unlikely to take place.

This is the most important stage. It decides the direction of each reaction. The more negative system produces electrons and moves to the left, Ag^+ reacts with Zn

See also Redox reactions of transition metal ions pp. 43

9 Organic chemistry

Basic concepts

Types of formula

Using ethanoic acid as an example:

- the *empirical* formula is CH_2O ⟶ The simplest, whole-number ratio of elements in a compound.
- the *molecular* formula is $C_2H_4O_2$ ⟶ The *actual* number of atoms of each element in a compound.
- the *structural* formula is CH_3COOH ⟶ The minimal detail, using conventional groups, for an unambiguous structure.
- the *displayed* formula is

$$H-\overset{\overset{\displaystyle H}{|}}{\underset{\underset{\displaystyle H}{|}}{C}}-C\overset{\displaystyle \nearrow O}{\underset{\displaystyle \searrow O-H}{}}$$

⟶ The relative placing of atoms and the bonds between them.

Functional groups

Organic chemistry is very much about reactions of functional groups.

Aliphatic compounds have a functional group attached to a comparatively unreactive carbon chain called an *alkyl* group:

Alkyl group – Unreactive carbon chain

Functional group – The part responsible for the reactions

$$H-\overset{\overset{\displaystyle H}{|}}{\underset{\underset{\displaystyle H}{|}}{C}}-\overset{\overset{\displaystyle H}{|}}{\underset{\underset{\displaystyle H}{|}}{C}}-\overset{\overset{\displaystyle H}{|}}{\underset{\underset{\displaystyle H}{|}}{C}}-X$$

- The alkyl group has the composition C_nH_{2n+1}
- Any alkyl group is represented as R–.
- Alkyl groups are derived from alkanes:

	Alkane		Alkyl group	
Number of carbons	Formula	Name	Formula	Name
1	CH_4	methane	CH_3	methyl
2	C_2H_6	ethane	C_2H_5	ethyl
3	C_3H_8	propane	C_3H_7	propyl
4	C_4H_{10}	butane	C_4H_9	butyl
5	C_5H_{12}	pentane	C_5H_{11}	pentyl
6	C_6H_{14}	hexane	C_6H_{13}	hexyl

Learn these

Aromatic compounds or *arenes* have a functional group next to an *aryl* group (a group containing a benzene ring):

Aryl group   or C_6H_5X

Functional group

An aryl group contains a benzene ring

- Any aryl group is often represented as Ar–.
- The simplest aryl group is the phenyl group, C_6H_5, derived from benzene, C_6H_6.

Common functional groups

It is essential that you can instantly identify a functional group within a molecule so that you can apply the relevant chemistry. You must learn all of these

name	functional group	examples		prefix or suffix (for naming)
alkane	C—H	$CH_3CH_2CH_3$ *propane*		-ane
alkene	C=C	CH_3CHCH_2 *propene*		-ene
halogeno-alkane	—Br	CH_3CH_2Br *bromoethane*	CH_3CH_2—Br	bromo-
alcohol	—OH	CH_3CH_2OH *ethanol*	CH_3CH_2—OH	-ol
aldehyde	—C(=O)H	CH_3CHO *ethanal*	H_3C—C(=O)H	-al
ketone	—C(=O)—	CH_3COCH_3 *propanone*	H_3C—C(=O)CH_3	-one
carboxylic acid	—C(=O)OH	CH_3COOH *ethanoic acid*	H_3C—C(=O)OH	-oic acid
ester	—C(=O)O—	CH_3COOCH_3 *methyl ethanoate*	H_3C—C(=O)O—CH_3	-oate
acyl chloride	—C(=O)Cl	CH_3COCl *ethanoyl chloride*	H_3C—C(=O)Cl	-oyl chloride
amine	—NH_2	$CH_3CH_2NH_2$ *ethylamine*	CH_3CH_2—NH_2	-amine
amide	—C(=O)NH_2	CH_3CONH_2 *ethanamide*	H_3C—C(=O)NH_2	-amide
nitrile	—C≡N	CH_3CN *ethanenitrile*	H_3C—CN	-nitrile

The alcohols have the general formula: $C_nH_{2n+1}OH$ Any alcohol can be represented as ROH

Homologous series

- A series of similar compounds with the same functional group.
- Each successive member differs by $-CH_2-$.
- Each member of the series reacts similarly.
- The *general formula* identifies *any* member of a homologous series.

The alcohols

CH_2 $\big\langle$ CH_3OH
CH_2 $\big\langle$ C_2H_5OH
$\big\langle$ C_3H_7OH

Same functional group, OH

See Functional groups pp. 85

Naming of organic compounds.

Names are always based upon the number of carbon atoms and the functional group. You must know the following rules before starting to name an organic compound.

Aliphatic compounds

Rule 1
The name is based upon the longest carbon chain length based on an **alkane**.

Rule 2
Any functional groups and alkyl groups are identified.
The names of any functional groups are added as a prefix, e.g. chloro- or suffix, e.g. -ol.

Rule 3
If there is more than one possibility then the carbon atoms are labelled with numbers. Lowest possible numbers are used throughout with the functional group taking the lowest.

Rule 4
If there is more than one alkyl or functional group, they are placed in alphabetical order.

Examples

2-methylbutan-1-ol

3-ethyl-4-methylpentan-2-one

Aromatic compounds

Aromatic compounds are numbered in a similar way. The benzene ring is numbered from the carbon atom attached to the functional group. However, the situation is more complicated: some compounds (e.g. hydrocarbons, carboxylic acids, aldehydes and ketones) are regarded as substituted benzene rings; other compounds (e.g. phenols, and amines) are considered as phenyl compounds, based upon C_6H_5.

You should be able to suggest names for simple arenes

benzene   1,3-dimethylbenzene   2,4,6-trichlorophenol

Characteristic organic reactions

Types of bond fission

An organic reaction involves **bond fission** (breaking of a covalent bond) followed by the formation of new bonds.
There are two types of bond fission possible:
- homolytic fission (free radical formation)
- heterolytic fission.

Homolytic fission
Bond-breaking produces two species of the same (*homo-*) type:
$$A:B \longrightarrow A\bullet + B\bullet$$
free radicals

These are very important principles, used throughout organic chemistry

Heterolytic fission

Bond-breaking produces two species of different (*hetero-*) type:

$$A\!:\!B \longrightarrow A\!:^- + B^+$$
$$\text{ions}$$

or

$$A\!:\!B \longrightarrow A^+ + B\!:^-$$
$$\text{ions}$$

Types of reagent

Free radical
- A species with an unpaired electron, often single atoms.
- Highly reactive.
- Reacts by pairing of an unpaired electron.
- Often involved in chain reactions.
- Examples: $Cl\bullet$, $CH_3\overset{\bullet}{}$.

Electrophile
- An electron-deficient species.
- Attacks a carbon atom that is electron-rich by **accepting a pair of electrons**.
- Examples: Br_2, HBr, H_2SO_4, NO_2^+ (nitronium ion)

Nucleophile
- An electron-rich species with a *lone pair of electrons*.
- Attacks a carbon atom that is electron-deficient by **donating a pair of electrons**.
- Examples: $:OH^-$, $:Br^-$, $:Cl^-$, $:NH_3$, $H_2O:$, $:CN^-$

Mechanisms

Remember that a curly arrow shows the movement of an electron pair

In mechanisms, a *curly arrow* is used to show the movement of **a pair of electrons**.
The curly arrow always goes **FROM** a nucleophile **TO** an electrophile.

attack by a nucleophile (e.g. Br^-) $:Br^-$

attack by an electrophile (e.g. NO_2^+) NO_2^+

breaking of a bond

$$-\!\!\overset{|}{\underset{|}{C}}\!-Br \longrightarrow -\!\!\overset{|}{\underset{|}{C}}{}^+ + :Br^-$$

the pair of electrons moves onto the bromine

Types of reaction

The main types of reaction are:
- substitution, addition, elimination, hydrolysis
- oxidation and reduction.

Substitution

Substitution: a swap

- A swapping over of one species for another,
  e.g. substitution of Br^- for OH^-:
$$CH_3Br + OH^- \longrightarrow CH_3OH + Br^-$$

Addition

Addition: 2 into 1

- Two species add together to make one.
- Usually produces: unsaturated compound $\longrightarrow$ saturated compound,
  e.g. addition of Br_2 to C_2H_4:
$$C_2H_4 + Br_2 \longrightarrow C_2H_4Br_2$$

Elimination:
1 into 2

Hydrolysis:
bond fission
involving water

When writing
equations in
organic
chemistry,
use [O] for an
oxidising
agent;
use [H] for a
reducing agent

See also: Polar
+ non-polar
molecules,
intermolecular
forces,
hydrogen
bonding pp.
23–26

Apply the
same
principles to
carboxylic
acids and
amines

Elimination

- One species breaks up to make two - the opposite to addition.
- Usually results in: saturated compound $\longrightarrow$ unsaturated compound,
  e.g. elimination of H_2O from C_2H_5OH:
  $$C_2H_5OH \longrightarrow C_2H_4 + H_2O$$

Hydrolysis

- A reaction where water breaks a bond
  e.g. hydrolysis of CH_3COOCH_3:
  $$CH_3COOCH_3 + H_2O \longrightarrow CH_3COOH + CH_3OH$$

Oxidation

- Gain of oxygen OR loss of hydrogen (accompanied by the loss of electrons to the organic compound)
  e.g. oxidation of C_2H_5OH:
  $$C_2H_5OH + [O] \longrightarrow CH_3CHO + H_2O$$

Reduction

- Loss of oxygen OR gain of hydrogen (accompanied by the gain of electrons to the organic compound)
  e.g. reduction of CH_3CHO:
  $$CH_3CHO + 2[H] \longrightarrow C_2H_5OH$$

Physical properties of organic compounds

Inductive effect

- The inductive effect results from a difference in electronegativity.
- This gives a polar molecule:

INDUCTIVE EFFECT   chlorine more electronegative than carbon - electron flow from carbon to chlorine - dipole produced

Non-polar compounds

Similar electronegativity of C and H means that hydrocarbons:
- are non-polar
- dissolve in non-polar solvents; insoluble in water.

Polar compounds

Organic molecules containing electronegative atoms of O, N or a halogen are polar.
- Alcohols, carboxylic acids and amines contain OH or NH groups. They are sufficiently polar to form hydrogen bonds,
  e.g. polarity in alcohols:

oxygen more electronegative than hydrogen dipole produced

Typical properties of polar organic compounds are:
- higher than expected melting and boiling points
- solubility in water (although this decreases rapidly with increasing chain length).

Short chain alcohols dissolve in water but solubility decreases as chain lengthens:

large polar
contribution

polar head

non-polar tail

most of the molecule
is a non-polar tail

polar head

non-polar tail

Melting point and boiling point within a homologous series C_5H_{12}

C_3H_8

Effect of chain length

Increasing chain length

m.pt and b. pt increase

more surface of contact between molecules
greater van der Waals' forces between molecules

C_5H_{12}

Isomers of C_4H_{10}

m.pt and b. pt increase

more surface of contact between molecules

greater van der Waals' forces between
molecules

Branching versus straight chains

Shapes of organic molecules, σ- and π-bonds

σ- and π-bonds are *molecular orbitals* that bond together the atoms in a molecule.
- In saturated compounds, all covalent bonds are σ-bonds.
- In unsaturated compounds, the double bond is made up of both a σ- and a π-bond.

σ-bonds:

- covalent bonds between C and H
- covalent bonds between C and C along the C-C axis
- formed by overlap of *s*- and *p*- atomic orbitals.

Bonding in methane, CH_4

The coverage here is greatly simplified but sufficient for most A-level syllabuses. Check to see if you need to know any more, particularly involving hybridisation

all σ-bonds

Tetrahedral molecule
4 electron pairs around carbon
bond-angle: 109.5°

π-bonds:

- the 'extra' covalent bond in a double bond (C=C and C=O)
- above and below the C–C axis
- formed by overlap of atomic *p*-orbitals.

Bonding in ethane, C_2H_4

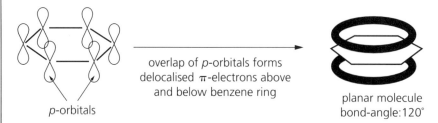

p-orbitals

overlap forms a π-bond

σ-bond

π-bond

The C=C bond
planar molecule
3 σ- electron pairs around C
bond-angle: approximately 120°

Delocalised bonding in benzene, C_6H_6

See also
'Arenes' for
evidence for a
delocalised
benzene
molecule

p-orbitals

overlap of *p*-orbitals forms
delocalised π-electrons above
and below benzene ring

planar molecule
bond-angle:120°

Isomerism

Structural isomerism

Structural isomers are molecules with the same molecular formula but with different structural arrangements of atoms.

Example The two structural isomers of C_4H_{10}:

Stereoisomerism

These are
relatively easy
exam marks.
Make sure
that you learn
this
thoroughly

Stereoisomers have the same structural formula but they differ by the position of atoms in space.
The two types of stereoisomerism are:
- *cis-trans* isomerism about a C=C double bond
- optical isomerism about a chiral carbon centre.

Cis-trans (or geometric) isomers
This isomerism occurs in a molecule with:
- a C=C double bond and
- two **different** groups attached to **each** carbon end of the double bond.

> **The π-bond of the double bond prevents rotation about the double bond.**

Example 1,2–dichloroethene has *cis-trans* isomers:

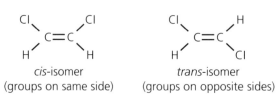

cis-isomer
(groups on same side)

trans-isomer
(groups on opposite sides)

Optical isomers

Optical isomers are organic molecules with a *chiral* centre, often as an *asymmetric* carbon atom.

> An **asymmetric** carbon atom has **four** different groups or atoms attached to it.

Optical isomers are mirror-image forms of one another.

Example The optical isomers of an amino acid, $RCHNH_2COOH$

chiral (or asymmetric) carbon atom

4 different groups attached

$$H_2N \overset{COOH}{\underset{H}{\overset{|}{C}}} R \qquad R \overset{COOH}{\underset{H}{\overset{|}{C}}} NH_2$$

mirror plane

Optical isomers or *'enantiomers'*:

- are identical chemically
- differ only by their rotation of plane-polarised light in opposite directions.

A synthetic amino acid, made in the laboratory, is optically inactive because it contains equal amounts of each optical isomer – a **racemic** mixture.

> *Draw optical isomers as 3–D structures. It is easiest to picture them as mirror images*

Hydrocarbons

Saturated and unsaturated hydrocarbons

- A saturated hydrocarbon has single bonds only.
- An unsaturated hydrocarbon contains a multiple carbon-carbon bond.
  Alkanes, C_nH_{2n+2} are saturated.
  Alkenes, C_nH_{2n}, with a double C=C bond, are unsaturated.

$$H-\overset{\overset{H}{|}}{\underset{\underset{H}{|}}{C}}-\overset{\overset{H}{|}}{\underset{\underset{H}{|}}{C}}-\overset{\overset{H}{|}}{\underset{\underset{H}{|}}{C}}-H \qquad \overset{H}{\underset{H}{\diagup}}C=C\overset{CH_3}{\underset{H}{\diagdown}}$$

saturated
single bonds only

unsaturated
contains a double bond

Hydrocarbons from oil

Crude oil is a source of hydrocarbons.
- Purification by fractional distillation.
- Subsequent processing by cracking and reforming.

Fractional distillation

- Separation of hydrocarbons into fractions according to their boiling points.
- The fractions are not pure and contain a mixture of hydrocarbons within a range of boiling points.

Cracking and reforming

Cracking and reforming can be used to obtain more useful alkanes and alkenes.

Cracking
- Breakdown of a saturated hydrocarbon into smaller hydrocarbons by heat.
- Catalyst (e.g. Al_2O_3) often used for lower temperatures, thus saving energy.
  Cracking results in an alkane and an alkene,
  e.g.   alkane $\longrightarrow$ alkane + alkene
  $$C_{10}H_{22} \longrightarrow C_8H_{18} + C_2H_4$$

> *Cracking is the starting point for the manufacture of many organics*

Reforming

- Used to obtain more useful hydrocarbons from fractions of little use.
- Heat and pressure required.
- Produces branched hydrocarbons.
- Produces cyclic hydrocarbons and arenes,
  e.g.   cyclohexane $\longrightarrow$ benzene + hydrogen

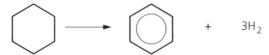

$+$ $3H_2$

Alkanes

General formula: C_nH_{2n+2}
- Non-polarity means that alkanes are generally unreactive towards nucleophiles and electrophiles.
- Few reactions.

Combustion

Combustion reactions of alkanes give their use as fuels.
Examples: $CH_4 + 2O_2 \longrightarrow CO_2 + 2H_2O$
                $2C_8H_{18} + 25O_2 \longrightarrow 16CO_2 + 18H_2O$

Environmental problems
- Lead, CO, NO_x and unburnt hydrocarbons in car emissions.
- Using catalytic converters and unleaded fuels reduces polluting gases.
- Excessive CO_2 emissions contributing to greenhouse effect.

Substitution

In the presence of u.v. radiation:
- substitution by chlorine and by bromine.
      $CH_4 + Cl_2 \longrightarrow CH_3Cl + HCl$
- free-radical process.

Mechanism of free-radical substitution

Initiation
Starts the reaction:
- u.v. radiation provides energy to break Cl–Cl bonds homolytically to produce chlorine free-radicals, $Cl\bullet$
      $Cl_2 \longrightarrow 2\ Cl\bullet$

Propagation
Makes the reaction products:
- free radicals are recycled - a chain reaction:

$$CH_4 + Cl\bullet \longrightarrow CH_3\bullet + HCl$$
$$CH_3\bullet + Cl_2 \longrightarrow CH_3Cl + Cl\bullet$$

Termination
Removes free radicals:
$$Cl\bullet + Cl\bullet \longrightarrow Cl_2$$
$$CH_3\bullet + Cl\bullet \longrightarrow CH_3Cl$$
$$CH_3\bullet + CH_3\bullet \longrightarrow CH_3CH_3$$

Impure products
Further substitution is possible, producing a mixture of products:

$$CH_3Cl \xrightarrow{Cl\bullet} CH_2Cl_2 \xrightarrow{Cl\bullet} CHCl_3 \xrightarrow{Cl\bullet} CCl_4$$

Alkenes

General formula: C_nH_{2n}

Addition reactions

- Electron density of π-bond attracts electrophiles.
- This allows addition across the double bond.
- The addition reaction with Br_2 is used as a test for unsaturation:

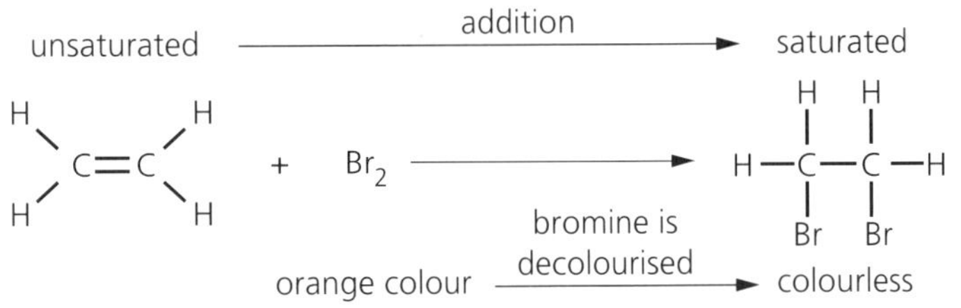

unsaturated   → addition →   saturated

bromine is decolourised

orange colour → colourless

Addition reactions of ethene

Addition reactions of alkenes are useful in organic synthesis.

For more details of poymerisation, see pp. 115–116

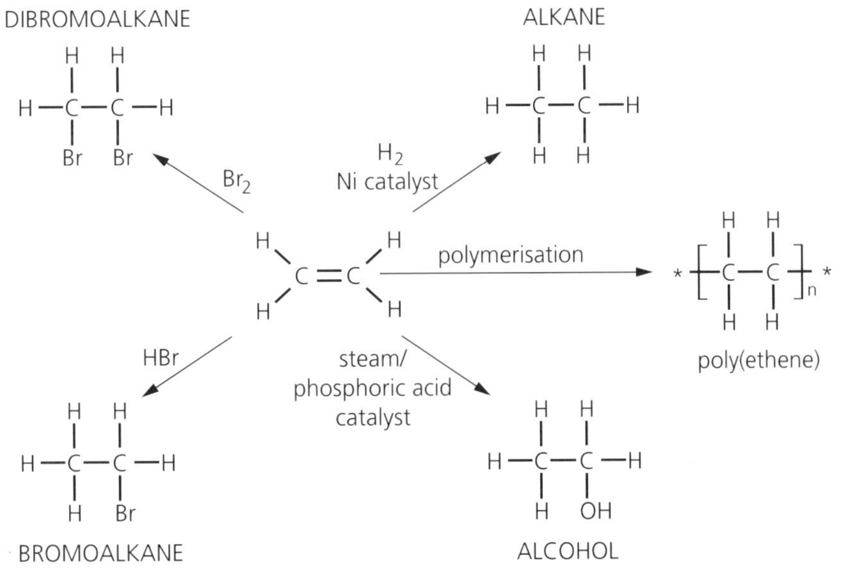

DIBROMOALKANE

Br_2

ALKANE

H_2 Ni catalyst

polymerisation

poly(ethene)

HBr

steam/ phosphoric acid catalyst

BROMOALKANE

ALCOHOL

Some syllabuses examine this reaction. Check yours

Note. An alternative synthesis of an alcohol from an alkene is:
- addition of concentrated sulphuric acid at room temperature,

$$C_2H_4 + H_2SO_4 \longrightarrow CH_3CH_2OSO_3H$$

- followed by hydrolysis,

$$CH_3CH_2OSO_3H + H_2O \longrightarrow CH_3CH_2OH + H_2SO_4$$

However, steam and phosphoric acid are used industrially.

Mechanism of electrophilic addition

Be careful with the direction of the curly arrows. Don't get confused by the charges and partial charges within this mechanism

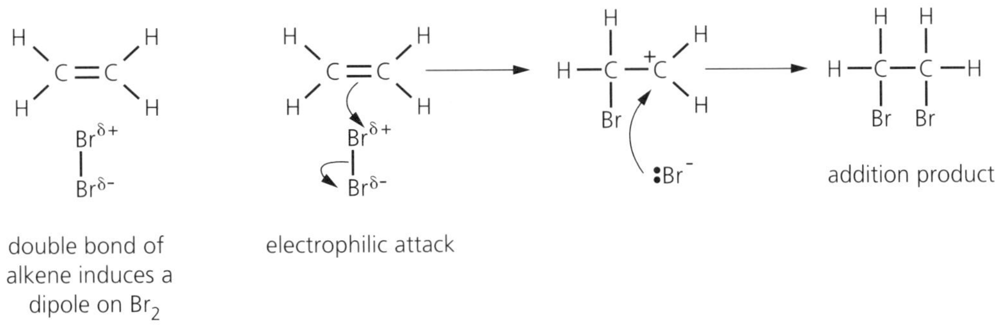

$Br^{\delta+}$
$Br^{\delta-}$

double bond of alkene induces a dipole on Br_2

$Br^{\delta+}$
$Br^{\delta-}$

electrophilic attack

$:Br^-$

addition product

Addition reactions of unsymmetrical alkenes

Example: The reaction of propene and HBr

Two products are possible: - the major product results from the more stable carbonium ion.

This is an important idea but not in all syllabuses. Check to see if you need to learn this. Your syllabus may also require this mechanism with H_2SO_4 – check

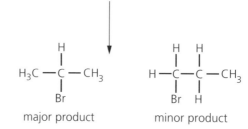

secondary carbonium ion

primary carbonium ion

electrophilic attack

secondary carbonium ion is more stable - inductive effect from two alkyl groups

major product

minor product

Oxidation reactions

Mild oxidation

Oxidation with cold, dilute acidified manganate(VII) to form a diol:

Remember to use [O] for the oxidising agent. Many candidates in exams get this reaction wrong by incorrectly adding Mn

$$H_2C=CH_2 + [O] + H_2O \xrightarrow[\text{cold}]{H^+/MnO_4^-}$$

ethane -1,2-diol

Strong oxidation

Conditions:

- hot, concentrated acidified manganate(VII)
- OR reductive ozonolysis.

Leads to the breaking of the carbon-carbon double bond ⟶ carbonyl compounds or carboxylic acids.

The C=C double bond breaks producing two C=O compounds.

Subsequent oxidation may occur to form a carboxylic acid

$$\xrightarrow[\text{reflux}]{H^+/MnO_4^-}$$

Arenes

- Arenes are compounds containing a benzene ring.

The bonding in benzene

Two structures are used to represent benzene, the modern delocalised structure being preferred.

See also 'Shapes of organic molecules' pp. 89–90

Kekulé structure

Alternating C=C and C-C bonds

Delocalised structure

Delocalised electrons
All carbon-carbon bonds identical

Evidence for delocalisation

Hydrogenation of cyclohexene

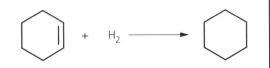

- 1 (C=C) bond reacts with H_2.
- Experimental value:
  $\Delta H^{\ominus} = -120$ kJ mol^{-1}

Hydrogenation of the Kekulé structure of benzene

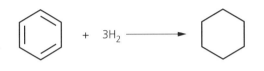

- 3 (C=C) bonds react with $3H_2$.
- The predicted value:
  $\Delta H^{\ominus} = 3 \times -120 = -360$ kJ mol^{-1}.
- The actual experimental value:
  $\Delta H^{\ominus} = -208$ kJ mol^{-1}.

- The difference above suggests that benzene has alternative, more stable bonding than that of the Kekulé structure.

Bond length data
- The Kekulé structure suggests 2 bond lengths: 0.134 nm and 0.154 nm.
- Experiment shows only one C–C bond length of 0.139 nm.

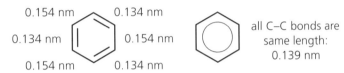

- This supports a model where all C–C bonds are between single and double bonds.

Comparing arenes with alkenes

Bonding
- Arenes and alkenes both have π-bonds, but **the electron density is less in arenes.**
- **The greater stability of arenes** results from the delocalised benzene ring compared with the localised electron density in alkenes.

Types of reaction
- Arenes and alkenes **both react with electrophiles**.
- The typical **reactions of arenes are substitution**: the benzene ring is preserved.
- The typical **reactions of alkenes are addition**: the double bond being removed.
- Arenes require more vigorous reaction conditions than alkenes.

Electrophilic substitution reactions of benzene

- The typical reaction of an arene is *electrophilic substitution*.
- The delocalised benzene ring attracts electrophiles.

Nitration of benzene

Arenes:
substitution

Alkenes:
addition

Although some heat (50°C) is required, too much may give further nitration of the benzene ring

Mechanism of electrophilic substitution in arenes
- The nitration mixture of concentrated HNO_3 and H_2SO_4 reacts to form the nitronium ion, NO_2^+

$$HNO_3 + H_2SO_4 \longrightarrow H_2NO_3^+ + HSO_4^-$$
$$H_2NO_3^+ \longrightarrow NO_2^+ + H_2O$$

- The powerful NO_2^+ electrophile then reacts with benzene:

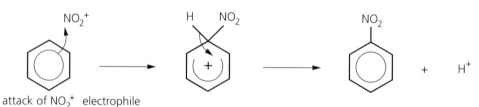

attack of NO_2^+ electrophile

- The H^+ formed regenerates a H_2SO_4 molecule:
$$H^+ + HSO_4^- \longrightarrow H_2SO_4$$
- H_2SO_4 acts as a catalyst.

Chlorination of benzene

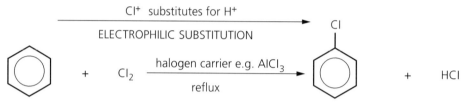

Typical 'halogen carriers' are:
- aluminium chloride, $AlCl_3$, or iron(III) chloride, $FeCl_3$, or Fe/Cl_2 (anhydrous conditions).
- the halogen carrier activates the chlorine forming the reactive chloronium ion, Cl^+:
$$Cl_2 + AlCl_3 \longrightarrow Cl^+ + AlCl_4^-$$
- this powerful Cl^+ electrophile reacts with benzene:

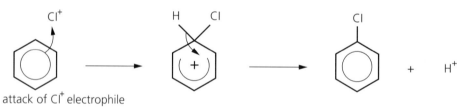

attack of Cl^+ electrophile

- the H^+ formed regenerates an $AlCl_3$ molecule:
$$H^+ + AlCl_4^- \longrightarrow AlCl_3 + HCl$$
- $AlCl_3$ acts as a catalyst.

Alkylation and acylation of benzene (Friedel-Crafts reaction)
- Very important reactions industrially.
- Similar principles and mechanisms to chlorination (e.g. use of halogen carrier).

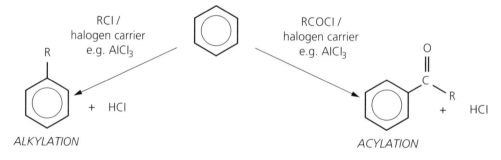

ALKYLATION   ACYLATION

Electrophilic substitution reactions of methylbenzene

Methylbenzene is slightly more reactive than benzene.
- The positive inductive effect of the methyl group increases the electron density of the benzene ring, particularly at the 2, 4 and 6 positions.
- Methylbenzene substitutes at the 2- and 4- positions.
- Reactions take place under milder conditions.

Note that milder conditions are required for the substitution of methylbenzene compared with benzene

Nitration and chlorination of methylbenzene

HNO$_3$ / H$_2$SO$_4$
room temperature

Cl$_2$ /AlCl$_3$, anhydrous conditions
room temperature

mixture of 2- and 4- substitution products

Chlorination of arenes in ultraviolet radiation

In ultraviolet light, chlorine reacts differently from the electrophilic substitution above.

Benzene in u.v. radiation

The chlorination of benzene and methylbenzene under different conditions produces different products

- **Addition** reaction to the benzene ring.
- Ultraviolet radiation (or strong sunlight) provides sufficient energy to break the delocalised ring of benzene.

Cl$_2$ / u.v. radiation

FREE-RADICAL **ADDITION**

Methylbenzene in u.v. radiation

Further chlorination of the side-chain gives a mixture of products (see also chlorination of alkanes pp. 92)

Substitution reaction **of the side-chain**.
Ultraviolet radiation (or strong sunlight) does **not** provide sufficient energy to break the delocalised ring of methylbenzene.

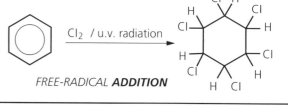

CH$_3$ Cl$_2$ / u.v. radiation   CH$_2$Cl   +   HCl

FREE-RADICAL **SUBSTITUTION**

Halogenoalkanes

General formula: C$_n$H$_{2n+1}$X;   R–X, where X = F, Cl, Br or I

Types of halogenoalkanes

1-bromopropane
primary

2-bromopropane
secondary

2-bromomethylpropane
tertiary

Polarity

The halogeno group, C–X, is polar:

electronegativity decreases from F to I

$$-\underset{/}{\overset{\backslash}{C}}\overset{\delta+}{-}\overset{\delta-}{F} \qquad -\underset{/}{\overset{\backslash}{C}}\overset{\delta+}{-}\overset{\delta-}{Cl} \qquad -\underset{/}{\overset{\backslash}{C}}\overset{\delta+}{-}\overset{\delta-}{Br} \qquad -\underset{/}{\overset{\backslash}{C}}\overset{\delta+}{-}\overset{\delta-}{I}$$

decreasing polarity ⟹

Halogenoalkanes:
- are **less polar** than alcohols
- **do not** mix with water and have **lower boiling points** than alcohols.

Nucleophilic substitution reactions

A common reaction of halogenoalkanes is **nucleophilic substitution** in which a nucleophile swaps over with a halogen.

The hydrolysis of halogenoalkanes

Reaction with aqueous hydroxide ions, $OH^-(aq) \longrightarrow$ ALCOHOL

$$C_2H_5Br + OH^-(aq) \xrightarrow[\text{reflux}]{OH^-/H_2O} C_2H_5OH + Br^-$$

Use NaOH(aq) as a source of OH⁻ (aq). The OH⁻ ion behaves as a nucleophile: donates an electron pair

- Primary halogenoalkanes are hydrolysed in a **one-step** mechanism:

- Tertiary halogenoalkanes are hydrolysed in a **two-step** mechanism:

In a tertiary halogenoalkane:
- there is a positive inductive effect from the **three** CH_3 groups
- the + charge on the intermediate carbonium ion is stabilised.

Comparing the hydrolysis of chloro-, bromo- and iodoalkanes

For the hydrolysis of halogenoalkanes, bond energy is more important than polarity

The rate of hydrolysis is compared using water in the presence of $AgNO_3(aq)$:

increasing rate of reaction ⟹

$$-\underset{/}{\overset{\backslash}{C}}\overset{\delta+}{-}\overset{\delta-}{F} \qquad -\underset{/}{\overset{\backslash}{C}}\overset{\delta+}{-}\overset{\delta-}{Cl} \qquad -\underset{/}{\overset{\backslash}{C}}\overset{\delta+}{-}\overset{\delta-}{Br} \qquad -\underset{/}{\overset{\backslash}{C}}\overset{\delta+}{-}\overset{\delta-}{I}$$

decreasing bond strength ⟹

The rate of hydrolysis increases as the C–X bond weakens.
- **Polarity** predicts that the C–F bond is most polar and would give the fastest reaction.
- **Bond energy** predicts that the C–I bond would be broken most easily and would give the fastest reaction.
- For this reaction, bond energies are more important than polarity.

Further examples of nucleophilic substitution

Halogenoalkanes are useful in synthesis

It is important that water is **not** present in these reactions or hydrolysis may take place. Ethanol is used as an alternative solvent:

(Note that HBr then reacts: $NH_3 + HBr \rightarrow NH_4Br$)

Increasing the carbon chain length
The length of a carbon chain can be increased by reacting a halogenoalkane with a cyanide, CN^- The resulting nitrile is easily **reduced** by a suitable reducing agent (e.g. Na in ethanol) to form an amine:

A carbon chain is lengthened by introducing a nitrile group

nitrile	+	reducing agent	$\longrightarrow$	amine
CH_3CH_2CN	+	4[H]		$CH_3CH_2CH_2NH_2$

Elimination reactions of halogenoalkanes

The OH^- ion behaves as a base: removes H^+ forming H_2O

An elimination reaction takes place when a halogenoalkane is heated with hydroxide ions in **anhydrous** conditions (using **ethanol** as a solvent).

Reaction with hydroxide ions, OH⁻/ethanol ⟶ ALKENE

Conditions
- Hydroxide ions, OH^- in ethanol, e.g. NaOH(ethanol).
- Reflux or boiling (78°C).

Elimination versus hydrolysis

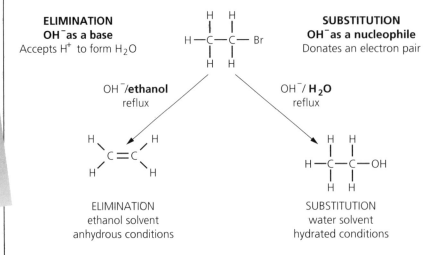

ELIMINATION
OH⁻ as a base
Accepts H^+ to form H_2O

SUBSTITUTION
OH⁻ as a nucleophile
Donates an electron pair

OH⁻/ethanol
reflux

OH⁻/ H_2O
reflux

ELIMINATION
ethanol solvent
anhydrous conditions

SUBSTITUTION
water solvent
hydrated conditions

Use different reaction conditions to control the type of reaction. Commonly tested in exams

Alcohols

General formula: $C_nH_{2n+1}OH$, ROH

Types of alcohols

primary alcohol

propan-1-ol

secondary alcohol

propan-2-ol

tertiary alcohol

methylpropan-2-ol

Polarity

The properties of alcohols are dominated by the hydroxyl group, C–OH

The hydroxyl group, C–OH, is polar:

- oxygen more electronegative than carbon and hydrogen
- dipole produced

Preparation of ethanol

Fermentation of sugars (for alcoholic drinks)
Yeast is added to an aqueous solution of sugar:
$$C_6H_{12}O_6 \longrightarrow 2C_2H_5OH + 2CO_2$$

Hydration of ethene (for industrial alcohol)
Ethene and steam are passed over a phosphoric acid catalyst at 180°C under high pressure:
$$C_2H_4 + H_2O \longrightarrow C_2H_5OH$$

Combustion of alcohols as fuels

$$C_2H_5OH + 3O_2 \longrightarrow 2CO_2 + 3H_2O$$

Reactions of alcohols with nucleophiles

A common reaction of alcohols is **nucleophilic substitution** in which a nucleophile swaps over with the hydroxyl group.

Reaction with bromide ions, Br⁻, in acid

$$C_2H_5OH \quad + \quad Br^- \ + \ H^+ \quad \longrightarrow \quad C_2H_5Br \quad + \quad H_2O$$

$$\text{H}-\overset{\overset{\text{H}}{|}}{\underset{\underset{\text{H}}{|}}{\text{C}}}-\overset{\overset{\text{H}}{|}}{\underset{\underset{\text{H}}{|}}{\text{C}}}-\text{OH} \xrightarrow[\text{reflux}]{\text{H}_2\text{SO}_4 \,/\, \text{NaBr}} \text{H}-\overset{\overset{\text{H}}{|}}{\underset{\underset{\text{H}}{|}}{\text{C}}}-\overset{\overset{\text{H}}{|}}{\underset{\underset{\text{H}}{|}}{\text{C}}}-\text{Br} \quad + \quad \text{H}_2\text{O}$$

- The polarity of the C–OH bond allows a reaction with a nucleophile such as Br⁻.
- The presence of an acid, H⁺ is essential
- The acid initially reacts with the alcohol forming a better leaving group:

gain of H⁺

'H₂O' is a better 'leaving group' than OH⁻

- Most reactions of alcohols require the presence of an acid

> *Use an acid with a nucleophile in substitution reactions of alcohols*

Oxidation of alcohols

Primary alcohols

primary alcohol ⟶ aldehyde ⟶ carboxylic acid
RCH₂OH ⟶ RCHO ⟶ RCOOH

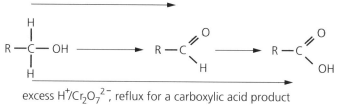

H⁺/Cr₂O₇²⁻, heat and distill immediately for an aldehyde product

excess H⁺/Cr₂O₇²⁻, reflux for a carboxylic acid product

> *The oxidation of different alcohols to give aldehydes, ketones and carboxylic acids is a crucial link in organic chemistry*

Conditions

A typical reagent is a mixture of:
- concentrated sulphuric acid, H₂SO₄ (source of H⁺)
- potassium dichromate, K₂Cr₂O₇ (source of Cr₂O₇²⁻)

$$CH_3CH_2OH \ + \ [O] \longrightarrow CH_3CHO \ + \ H_2O$$

> *For balanced equations, the oxidising agent can be shown simply as [O]*

Secondary alcohols

Oxidation is only possible to the ketone stage.
secondary alcohol ⟶ ketone
R₂CHOH ⟶ R₂CO

$$\text{R}-\overset{\overset{\text{H}}{|}}{\underset{\underset{\text{R}}{|}}{\text{C}}}-\text{OH} \xrightarrow[\text{heat}]{\text{H}^+/\text{Cr}_2\text{O}_7{}^{2-}} \text{R}-\text{C}\overset{O}{\underset{R}{\diagup\!\!\diagdown}} \longrightarrow \text{NO FURTHER OXIDATION}$$

> *The orange dichromate ions, Cr₂O₇²⁻, are reduced to green Cr³⁺ ions*

Tertiary alcohols

No oxidation is possible under normal conditions.

Formation of esters

Esters from a carboxylic acid and an alcohol. For more details, see 'Carboxylic acids' pp. 106–107

carboxylic acid + alcohol $\longrightarrow$ ester + water

CH_3COOH + CH_3OH $\longrightarrow$ CH_3COOCH_3 + H_2O

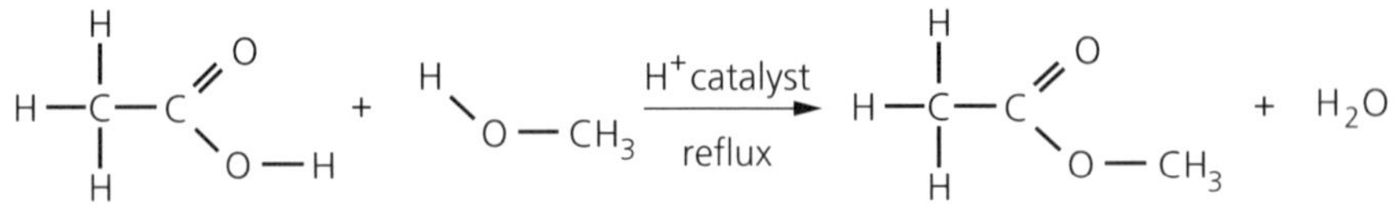

Dehydration of alcohols

An elimination reaction

C_2H_5OH $\longrightarrow$ C_2H_4 + H_2O

Conditions

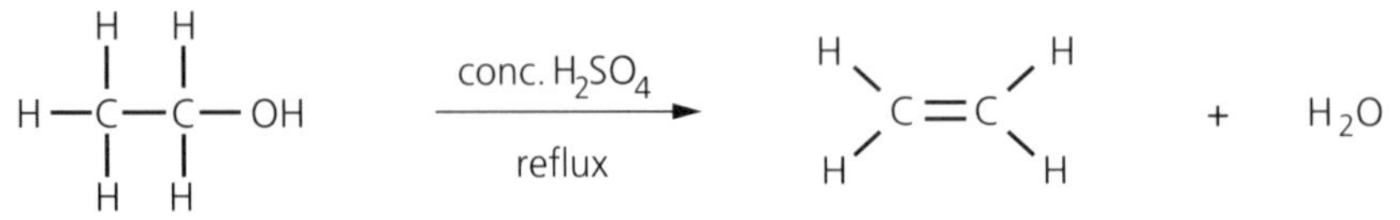

Use hot concentrated acid for elimination of water from an alcohol

- Concentrated acid catalyst, H^+ (e.g. conc H_2SO_4 or phosphoric acid H_3PO_4).
- Reflux or boiling.

Role of the acid catalyst

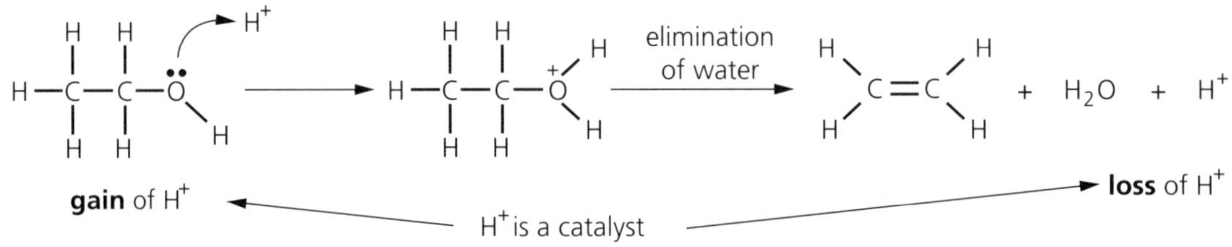

Tests for the hydroxyl group

Reaction with sodium
Alcohols react with sodium, releasing hydrogen gas.

Sodium releases H_2 from any compound with a hydroxyl group: alcohols, carboxylic acids (and water)

ethanol + sodium $\longrightarrow$ sodium ethoxide + hydrogen gas

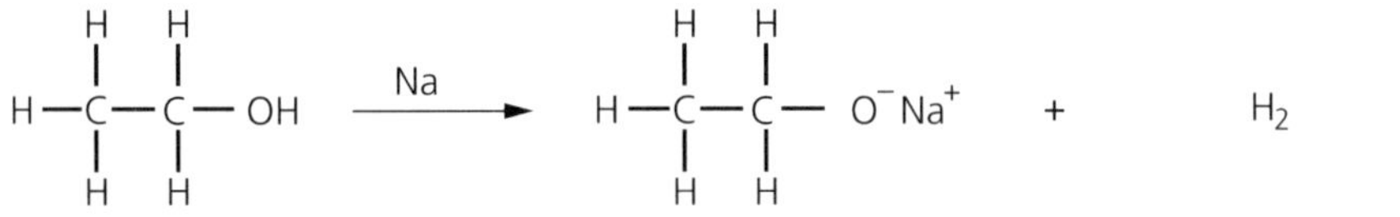

$2C_2H_5OH + 2Na \longrightarrow 2C_2H_5O^-Na^+ + H_2$

Reaction with phosphorus pentachloride
Alcohols react with PCl_5, releasing hydrogen chloride gas which forms misty fumes in air.

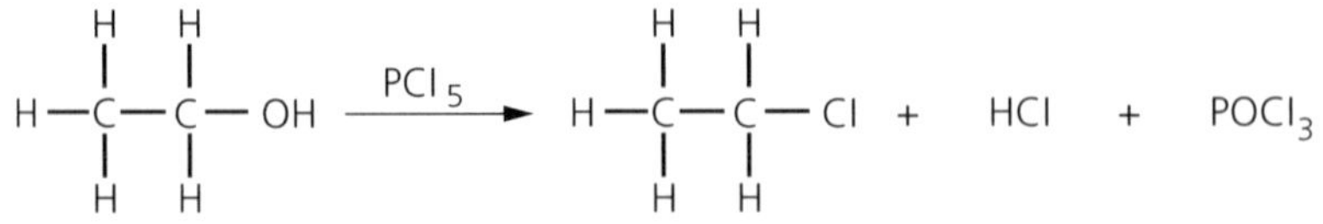

Learn these tests

$C_2H_5OH + PCl_5 \longrightarrow C_2H_5Cl + HCl + POCl_3$

In the presence of ammonia, the HCl gas forms dense white fumes of ammonium chloride:

$NH_3 + HCl \longrightarrow NH_4Cl$

Carbonyl compounds

General formula: $C_nH_{2n}O$

aldehyde, RCHO

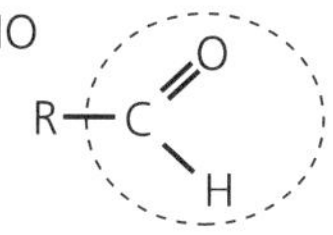

ketone, RCOR'

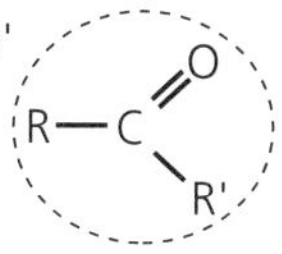

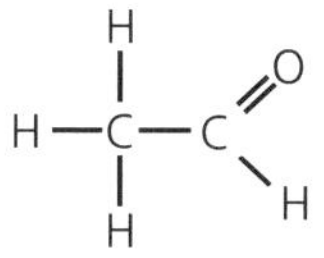

ethanal

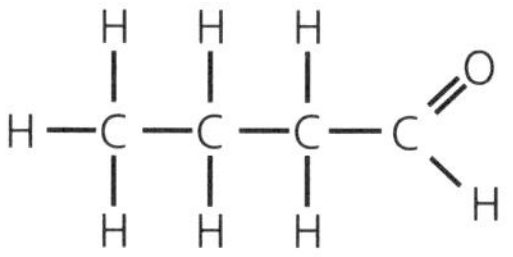

butanal

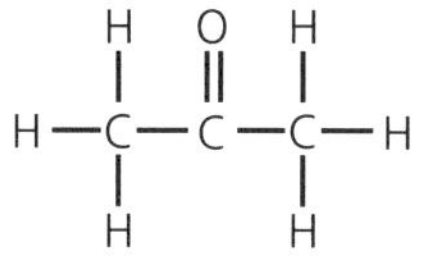

propanone

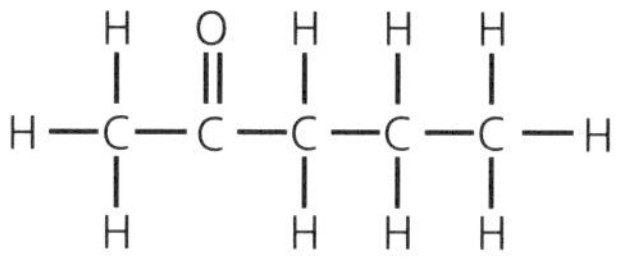

pentan-2-one

Polarity

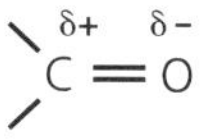

$$\overset{\delta+}{C} = \overset{\delta-}{O}$$ oxygen more electronegative than carbon
dipole produced

The carbonyl group, C=O, is polar, but less so than the hydroxyl group, C−OH in alcohols.

Carbonyl compounds produce an orange-yellow crystalline solid

Identification tests

Test for the presence of a carbonyl group

Brady's reagent
Brady's reagent is 2,4-dinitrophenylhydrazine (2,4-DNPH) in dilute acid.

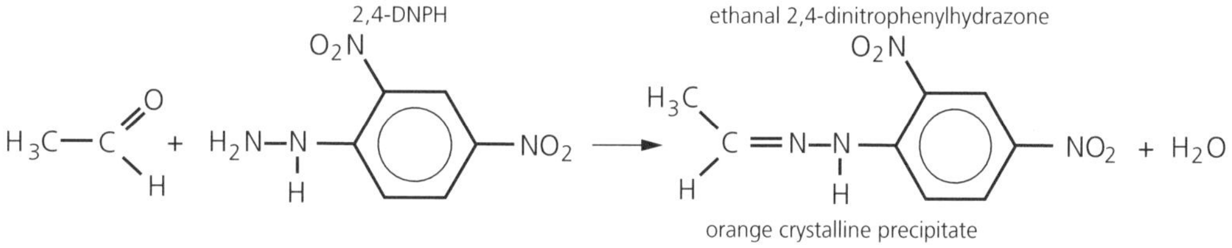

2,4-DNPH

ethanal 2,4-dinitrophenylhydrazone

orange crystalline precipitate

This is a *condensation reaction* − water is lost.

2,4-DNPH 'derivatives' of carbonyl compounds (aldehydes and ketones) are important in organic analysis.

- The bright orange-yellow crystals identify the carbonyl group (C=O group).
- The crystals have very sharp melting points. This melting point can be compared with known melting points from databases − the carbonyl compound can be identified.

Tests for aldehydes

- These tests rely on the oxidation of an aldehyde to a carboxylic acid.

The oxidising agent that is used changes colour as it is reduced (see below for details).

Ketones cannot be oxidised and they do not react with either Tollen's reagent or Fehling's solution

Tollen's reagent
Tollen's reagent is silver nitrate in aqueous ammonia.

Aldehydes produce a silver mirror by reduction of silver ions to silver:
$Ag^+ (aq) + e^- \longrightarrow Ag(s)$

Fehling's solution or Benedict's solution
Fehling's solution or Benedict's solution is an alkaline solution containing Cu^{2+} (aq) ions

> Aldehydes produce a brick-red precipitate of Cu_2O.
> The copper(II) ions, Cu^{2+}, are **reduced** to copper (I) ions, Cu^+:
> $2Cu^{2+}(aq) + 2e^- + 2OH^-(aq) \longrightarrow Cu_2O(s) + H_2O(l)$

Test for a methyl carbonyl compound

The triiodomethane (iodoform) reaction
The compound is heated with iodine, I_2, in aqueous sodium hydroxide, OH^- (aq).

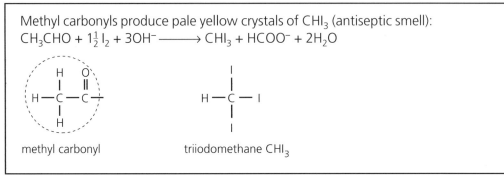

> Methyl carbonyls produce pale yellow crystals of CHI_3 (antiseptic smell):
> $CH_3CHO + 1\frac{1}{2}I_2 + 3OH^- \longrightarrow CHI_3 + HCOO^- + 2H_2O$
>
> methyl carbonyl   triiodomethane CHI_3

Note
- The mixture of I_2/OH^- oxidises alcohols to aldehydes or ketones.
- The triiodomethane reaction is also positive with alcohols that can be oxidised to methyl carbonyls:
  i.e. alcohols of this type, CH_3CHOH:

Summary of carbonyl tests

test	observation	conclusion
2,4-DNPH *(Brady's reagent)*	yellow-orange crystals	carbonyl group present: aldehyde **or** ketone
Ag^+/NH_3 *(Tollen's reagent)*	silver mirror	aldehyde present
Cu^{2+}/OH^- *(Fehling's or Benedict's solution)*	brick-red precipitate	aldehyde present
I_2/OH^- *(aqueous alkaline iodine)*	pale-yellow crystals with antiseptic smell	methyl carbonyl present **OR** alcohols with CH_3CHOH

Reduction of carbonyl compounds

Carbonyl compounds are reduced to alcohols using a suitable reducing agent such as hydrogen, H_2, and a nickel catalyst:

> aldehyde $\quad + \quad H_2 \longrightarrow$ primary alcohol
> $\quad CH_3CHO \quad + \quad H_2 \longrightarrow CH_3CH_2OH$
>
> ketone $\quad + \quad H_2 \longrightarrow$ secondary alcohol
> $\quad C_2H_5COCH_3 \quad + \quad H_2 \longrightarrow C_2H_5CH(OH)CH_3$

Other suitable reducing agents are:
- lithium aluminium hydride, $LiAlH_4$ in dry ether (at room temperature)
- sodium borohydride, $NaBH_4$ in dry ether (at room temperature).

For balanced equations, the reducing agent can be shown simply as [H]:
$$CH_3CHO + 2[H] \longrightarrow CH_3CH_2OH$$

Nucleophilic addition of hydrogen cyanide, HCN

aldehyde + HCN $\longrightarrow$ hydroxynitrile

CH_3CHO + HCN $\longrightarrow$ $CH_3CH(OH)CN$

HCN is added across the C=O double bond

Mechanism

Increasing the carbon chain length

- This reaction is useful for increasing the length of a carbon chain.
- Nitriles are easily *hydrolysed* by water in hot dilute acid to form a carboxylic acid.
- Nitriles are easily *reduced* by sodium in ethanol to form an amine.

Carboxylic acids

General formula: $C_nH_{2n+1}COOH$, $RCOOH$

Polarity

carboxyl group

The hydroxyl group, –OH, **and** the carbonyl group, C=O make the carboxylic acid molecule more polar than either alcohols or carbonyl compounds.

Carboxylic acids as 'acids'

Carboxylic acids are weak acids because they only partially dissociate:

carboxylic acid $\rightleftharpoons$ carboxylate ion + proton
$CH_3COOH \rightleftharpoons CH_3COO^- + H^+$

- Only 1 molecule in about 100 actually dissociates.
- Only a small proportion of the potential H^+ ions are released.

The carboxylate ion

The carboxylate ion is formed whenever a carboxylic acid is added to an alkali:

carboxylic acids exist
in acidic conditions

carboxylates exist
in alkaline conditions

Acid reactions of carboxylic acids

- Reaction with an alkali forms a salt and water only:

acid	+	alkali	$\longrightarrow$	salt	+	water
CH_3COOH	+	NaOH	$\longrightarrow$	CH_3COONa	+	H_2O
ethanoic acid				sodium ethanoate		

- Reaction with a metal forms a salt and hydrogen gas:

acid	+	metal	$\longrightarrow$	salt	+	hydrogen
$2CH_3COOH$	+	Mg	$\longrightarrow$	$(CH_3COO)_2Mg$	+	H_2
ethanoic acid				magnesium ethanoate		

- Reaction with a carbonate forms a salt, carbon dioxide and water:

acid	+	carbonate	$\longrightarrow$	salt	+	carbon dioxide	+	wate
$2CH_3COOH$	+	$CaCO_3$	$\longrightarrow$	$(CH_3COO)_2Ca$	+	CO_2	+	H_2O
ethanoic acid				calcium ethanoate				

Ethanoic acid, CH_3COOH, (vinegar) is the commonest and most useful of the carboxylic acids

Carboxylic acids are the 'organic acids'

See also 'Acids and Bases', pp. 62–68

Carboxylic acids react by the usual 'acid reactions':

Preparation of carboxylic acids

Oxidation of alcohols or aldehydes

Reflux with an excess of an oxidising agent:

> *from a primary alcohol:* $CH_3CH_2OH + 2[O] \longrightarrow CH_3COOH + H_2O$
> *from an aldehyde:* $\quad\quad CH_3CHO + [O] \longrightarrow CH_3COOH$

The common oxidising agent used is $H_2SO_4/K_2Cr_2O_7$

Hydrolysis of nitriles

Nitriles are easily *hydrolysed* by water
- in hot dilute acid to form a carboxylic acid:

> $\quad$ NITRILE $\quad\xrightarrow{\text{acid hydrolysis}}\quad$ CARBOXYLIC ACID
> $CH_3CH_2CN \quad + \quad 2H_2O + H^+ \longrightarrow \quad CH_3CH_2COOH \quad + \quad NH_4^+$

- or in hot aqueous alkali to form a carboxylate ion:

> $\quad$ NITRILE $\quad\xrightarrow{\text{alkali hydrolysis}}\quad$ CARBOXYLATE
> $CH_3CH_2CN \quad + \quad H_2O + OH^- \longrightarrow \quad CH_3CH_2COO^- \quad + \quad NH_3$
> A carboxylic acid is formed by adding dilute aqueous acid to the carboxylate:
> $CH_3CH_2COO^- + H^+ \longrightarrow CH_3CH_2COOH$

Carboxylic acid derivatives

- Compounds that can be made from carboxylic acids.

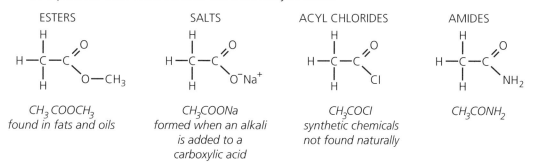

ESTERS

CH_3COOCH_3
found in fats and oils

SALTS

CH_3COONa
formed when an alkali
is added to a
carboxylic acid

ACYL CHLORIDES

CH_3COCl
synthetic chemicals
not found naturally

AMIDES

CH_3CONH_2

Carboxylates: salts of carboxylic acids

Carboxylic acid salts, 'carboxylates', are **ionic** compounds containing ions that are bonded by electrostatic forces.

CH_3COONa
sodium ethanoate

Properties
Carboxylates:
- are solids at room temperature with high melting and boiling points
- have a giant lattice structure
- dissolve in water and totally dissociate into ions.

Esters

General formula: RCOOR'

Naming esters

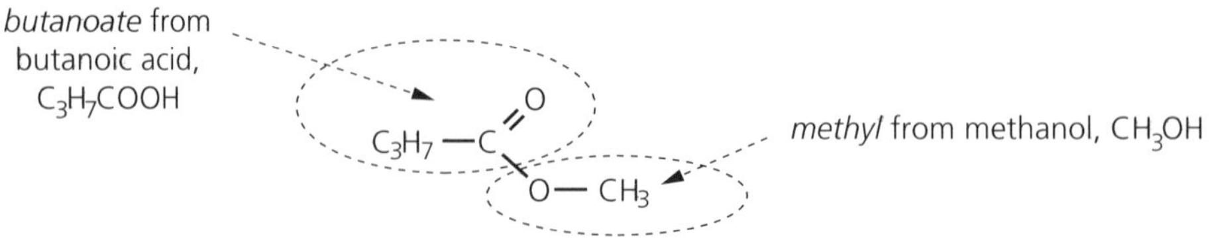

butanoate from butanoic acid, C_3H_7COOH

$C_3H_7 - C$ with =O and O—CH_3

methyl from methanol, CH_3OH

methyl butanoate

- The *alcohol* part comes first as the ....*yl:*   methyl
- The carboxylic acid part comes second as the ....*oate:*   butanoate

Formation of esters

Esterification is the formation of an **ester** from a *carboxylic acid* and an *alcohol:*

carboxylic acid   +   alcohol $\longrightarrow$ ester   +   water

CH_3COOH + CH_3OH $\longrightarrow$ CH_3COOCH_3 + H_2O

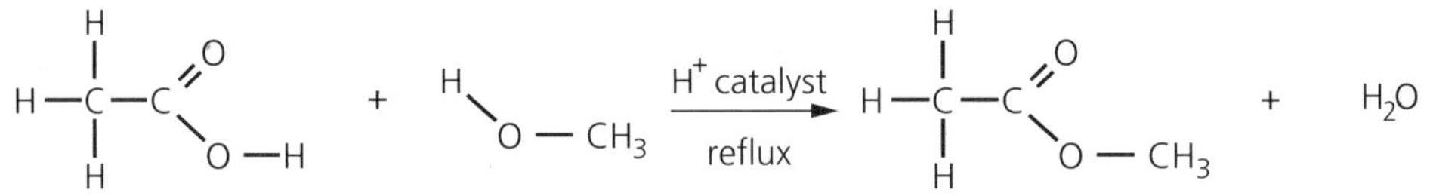

ethanoic acid   +   methanol $\longrightarrow$ methyl ethanoate   +   water

(reaction: H^+ catalyst, reflux, + H_2O)

Conditions

- An acid catalyst (a few drops of conc. H_2SO_4) and reflux.
- The yield is usually poor due to incomplete reaction.

Hydrolysis of esters

Hydrolysis is the breaking down of a compound using water: **water is a reactant**.

ester   +   water $\underset{\text{esterification}}{\overset{\text{hydrolysis}}{\rightleftharpoons}}$ carboxylic acid   +   alcohol

Esterification is the reverse reaction to the hydrolysis of esters: **water is a product**.

Hydrolysis breaks down an ester into an alcohol and its:
- carboxylic acid (acid hydrolysis) or
- carboxylate (alkali hydrolysis).

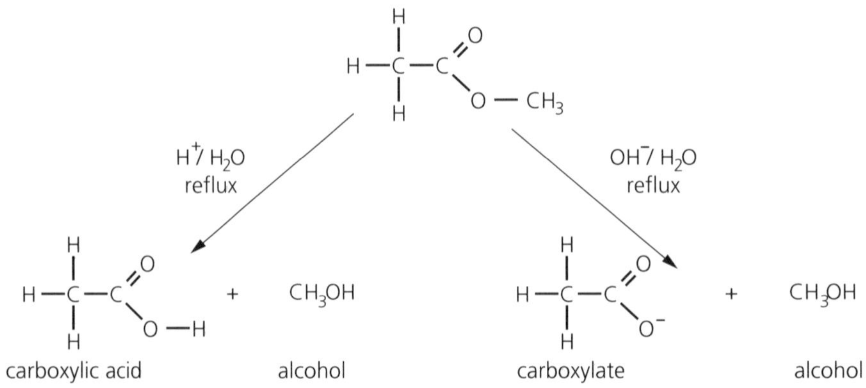

H^+/H_2O reflux

OH^-/H_2O reflux

carboxylic acid   + CH_3OH alcohol

carboxylate   + CH_3OH alcohol

ACID HYDROLYSIS

ALKALINE HYDROLYSIS

Acyl chlorides

General formula: $C_nH_{2n+1}COCl$,   RCOCl

The COCl group is the functional group of an *acyl chloride:*

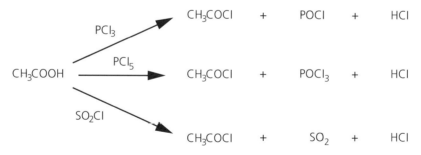

ethanoyl chloride   benzoyl chloride

Properties
Acyl chlorides are the most reactive organic compounds that are commonly used.

The relatively large $\delta+$
charge attracts the lone
pair of a nucleophile

The electron-withdrawing effects of both the **chlorine** atom and carbonyl **oxygen** atom produces a relatively large $\delta+$ charge on the carbonyl carbon atom.

Acyl chlorides in organic synthesis
The high reactivity of acyl chlorides compared with carboxylic acids makes them particularly useful in organic synthesis of related compounds.

Advantages:
- good yield of product
- reaction often occurs quickly and at room temperature.

Preparation of acyl chlorides

The high reactivity of acyl chlorides means that they are usually prepared from the parent carboxylic acid *'in situ'*, i.e. when they are needed.

Reagents
Phosphorus chlorides (PCl_3 or PCl_5) or SO_2Cl

CH_3COOH

PCl_3 → CH_3COCl + POCl + HCl

PCl_5 → CH_3COCl + $POCl_3$ + HCl

SO_2Cl → CH_3COCl + SO_2 + HCl

Reactions of acyl chlorides with nucleophiles
Conditions
- The required nucleophile is added to the acyl chloride.
- Anhydrous conditions are **essential** - acyl chlorides react with water.

lone pair attracted to $C^{\delta+}$

nucleophile

HCl forms

Nucleophiles of the type HY: react readily with acyl chlorides.
     RCOCl + HY ———→ RCOY + HCl

This is an **addition-elimination** reaction involving:
- addition of HY across the C=O double bond followed by
- elimination of HCl.

Summary of reactions with nucleophiles

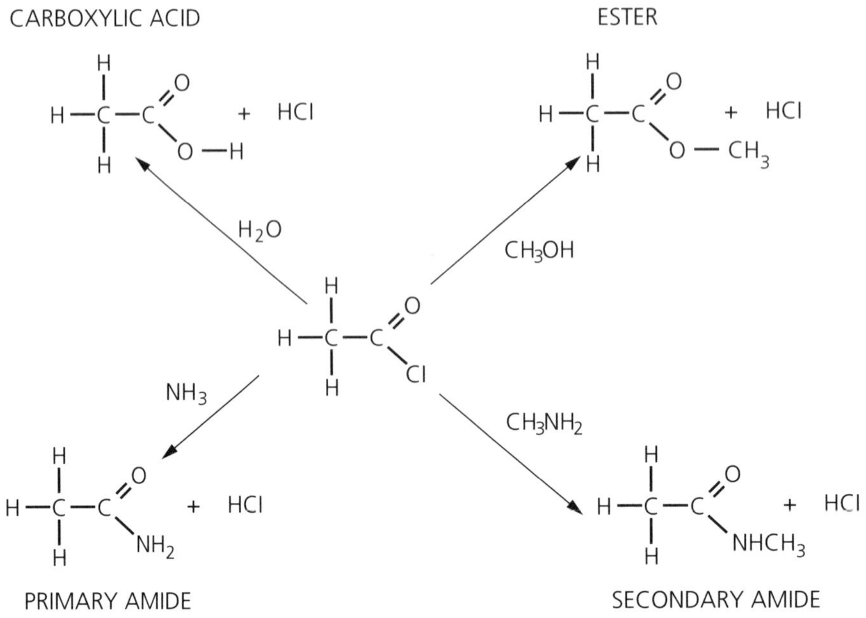

CARBOXYLIC ACID

ESTER

PRIMARY AMIDE

SECONDARY AMIDE

Note: In reactions with NH_3, the HCl reacts: $NH_3 + HCl \longrightarrow NH_4Cl$

- Hydrogen chloride is formed in all reactions of an acyl chloride with a nucleophile.
- Reactions take place at room temperature.
- Acyl chlorides are the only common organic compounds that react violently with water.

Acid anhydrides

Acyl chlorides are ideal for small-scale preparations in the laboratory. They are too expensive and too reactive for large-scale preparations for which they are replaced by acid anhydrides:

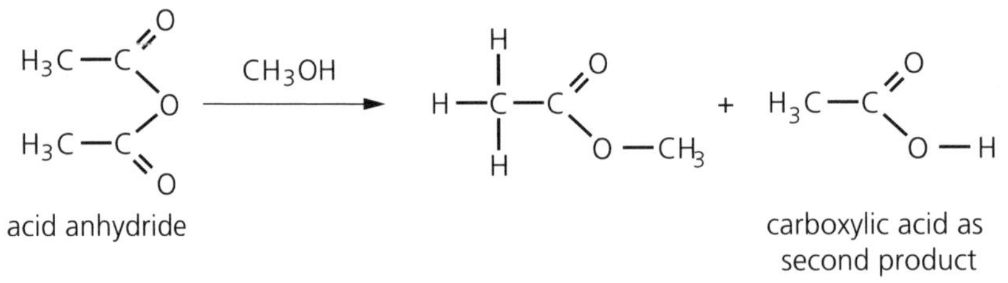

acid anhydride

carboxylic acid as
second product

- The reaction is slower and easier to control on a large scale.
- The same essential reaction as with an acyl chloride, but RCOOH forms instead of HCl as the second product.

Organic nitrogen compounds

Amines

General formula: RNH_2

Types of amines

primary amine	secondary amine	tertiary amine	aromatic amine

$$H-\underset{\underset{H}{|}}{\overset{\overset{H}{|}}{C}}-\underset{\underset{H}{|}}{\overset{\overset{H}{|}}{C}}-NH_2$$

$$H-\underset{\underset{H}{|}}{\overset{\overset{H}{|}}{C}}-\underset{\underset{H}{|}}{\overset{\overset{H}{|}}{C}}-NHCH_3$$

$$H-\underset{\underset{H}{|}}{\overset{\overset{H}{|}}{C}}-\underset{\underset{H}{|}}{\overset{\overset{H}{|}}{C}}-N(CH_3)_2$$

phenylamine $-NH_2$

ethylamine　　　　*N*-methylethylamine　　　　*N,N*-dimethylethylamine　　　　phenylamine

Amines as bases

> Amines are the organic bases

The basic strength of a compound depends upon the ability of the nitrogen atom to **accept** a proton, H^+.
For a primary amine:

- $RNH_2 + H^+ \rightleftharpoons RNH_3^+$

> The basic strength depends upon the availability of the nitrogen lone pair

Basicity of methylamine, ammonia and phenylamine
Electron-withdrawing groups, e.g. C_6H_5, **decrease** the basic strength.
Electron-donating groups, e.g. alkyl groups, **increase** the basic strength.

inductive effect causes electron flow away from nitrogen
◄————————

decrease in electron density of nitrogen lone pair

inductive effect causes electron flow towards nitrogen
————————►

increase in electron density of nitrogen lone pair

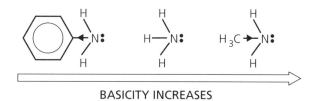

BASICITY INCREASES

Preparation of amines

Preparation of aliphatic amines from nitriles
A nitrile can be *reduced* with a suitable reducing agent (e.g. Na in ethanol) to form an amine:

$$CH_3CH_2CN \quad + \quad 4[H] \quad \longrightarrow \quad CH_3CH_2CH_2NH_2$$

> Other reducing agents: $LiAlH_4$ in dry ether (anhydrous conditions) is an almost universal reducing agent and works in most organic reductions

$$H-\underset{\underset{H}{|}}{\overset{\overset{H}{|}}{C}}-\underset{\underset{H}{|}}{\overset{\overset{H}{|}}{C}}-C\equiv N \quad + \quad 4[H] \quad \xrightarrow{Na/ethanol} \quad H-\underset{\underset{H}{|}}{\overset{\overset{H}{|}}{C}}-\underset{\underset{H}{|}}{\overset{\overset{H}{|}}{C}}-\underset{\underset{H}{|}}{\overset{\overset{H}{|}}{C}}-NH_2$$

Preparation of aromatic amines from an aromatic nitro compound
Nitrobenzene can be *reduced* with a suitable reducing agent (e.g. Sn in conc HCl) to form phenylamine.

$$C_6H_5NO_2 \quad + \quad 6[H] \quad \longrightarrow \quad C_6H_5NH_2 \quad + \quad 2H_2O$$

$$\bigcirc\!\!-NO_2 \quad + \quad 6[H] \quad \xrightarrow[reflux]{Sn/conc\ HCl} \quad \bigcirc\!\!-NH_2 \quad + \quad 2H_2O$$

phenylamine

Formation of azo dyes

An important process, forming the basis for the production of many modern-day dyestuffs.

Diazonium salts
Prepared by adding HNO_2/HCl to an aromatic amine such as phenylamine.

Nitrous acid, HNO_2, is unstable and is prepared *in situ* from $NaNO_2$ and HCl:

$$NaNO_2 + HCl \longrightarrow HNO_2 + NaCl$$

The nitrous acid then reacts with phenylamine

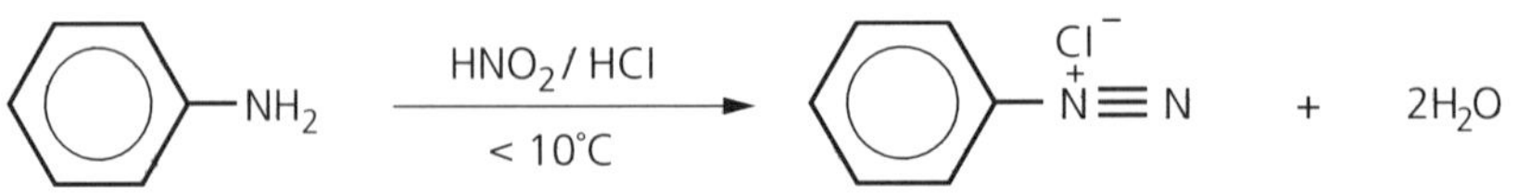

benzenediazonium chloride
(diazonium salt)

$$C_6H_5NH_2 + HNO_2 + HCl \longrightarrow C_6H_5N_2^+Cl^- + 2H_2O$$

- Aromatic diazonium salts are stable below 10°C.
- Aliphatic diazonium salts are unstable.

Azo dyes
A suitable aromatic compound is coupled with the diazonium salt in aqueous alkali to produce an azo dye,

e.g. with phenol:

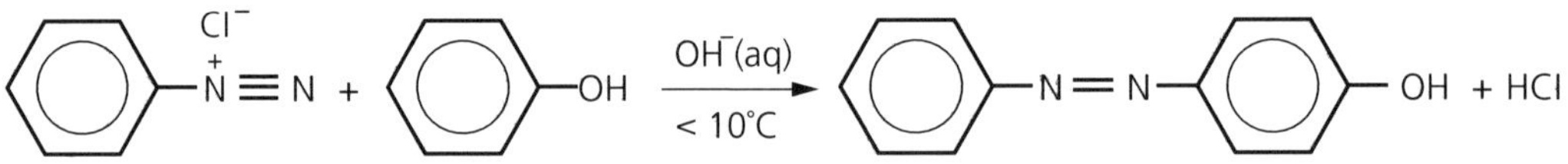

azo dye

- The azo dye is coloured.
- Coupling with aromatic compounds forms different coloured dyes.
- The reaction is reversible. The OH⁻ removes the HCl as it forms and this moves the equilibrium in favour of the products.

Amides

General formula: $RCONH_2$

Types of amides

primary amide   secondary amide   tertiary amide

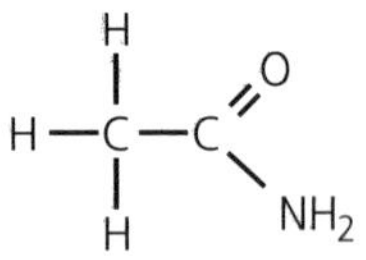

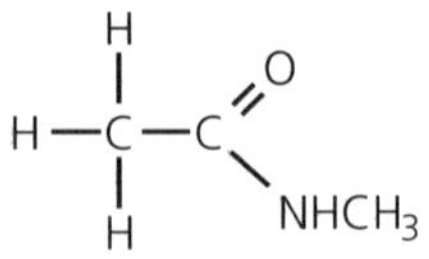

ethanamide   *N*-methylethanamide   *N*,*N*-dimethylethanamide

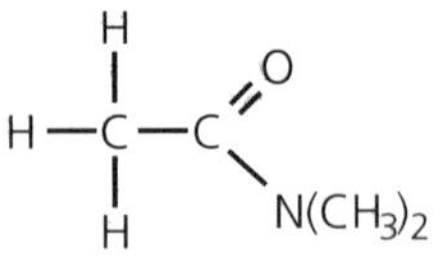

Properties

- Very weak organic bases.
- Relatively stable organic compounds.
- Polar compounds but insoluble in water, soluble in organic solvents.
- Relatively high melting points owing to H-bonding between molecules.

See also 'Acyl chlorides', pp. 109

Preparation of amides

Prepared by the reaction of an acyl chloride with ammonia or amines,

e.g. $CH_3COCl + NH_3 \longrightarrow CH_3CONH_2 + HCl$

(followed by: $NH_3 + HCl \longrightarrow NH_4Cl$)

Hydrolysis of amides

Note the different hydrolysis product from acid hydrolysis and alkali hydrolysis

Hydrolysis breaks down a primary amide to its parent carboxylic acid (acid hydrolysis) or carboxylate (alkali hydrolysis).

carboxylic acid   ammonium ion   carboxylate   ammonia

ACID HYDROLYSIS   ALKALINE HYDROLYSIS

Amino acids

There are 22 naturally occurring amino acids

General formula: $RCHNH_2COOH$

Properties

Amino acid molecules:
- contain the amino group, NH_2 – a base
- contain the carboxyl group, $COOH$ – an acid
- are soluble in water and in both acids and alkalis.

At the isoelectric point, the amino acid molecules exist in equilibrium with their zwitterions

Amino acids in aqueous solution

Each amino acid has a particular pH called the *isoelectric point* at which the overall charge is zero, e.g. the isoelectric point of glycine, CH_2NH_2COOH, is pH = 6.0

zwitterion: two ions in one molecule

At a pH more acidic than the isoelectric point, the amino acid forms a positive ion:

An amino acid exists in different ionic forms at pHs different from its isoelectric point.

At a pH more alkaline than the isoelectric point, the amino acid forms a negative ion:

ACIDIC CONDITIONS   ALKALINE CONDITIONS

Melting point
Solid amino acids exist partly as *zwitterions* that:
- attract one another strongly
- give amino acids a higher melting point than would otherwise be expected.

Optical isomers
All amino acids except aminoethanoic acid, glycine, H_2NCH_2COOH, are optically active.

See 'Optical isomers', pp. 91

Natural products

Proteins

- A protein is a chain of many amino acids linked by 'peptide bonds'.
- A protein is formed from amino acids by **condensation polymerisation** - involves loss of water,

e.g. the condensation of the amino acid glycine with alanine, forming a dipeptide:

A protein is formed by condensation polymerisation of amino acids

glycine *alanine* *peptide link*

- Addition of further amino acids builds up a *polypeptide or protein.*
- One water molecule is eliminated for each amino acid added to the chain.
- The 'peptide link' is CONH.

Hydrolysis of proteins

See 'Hydrolysis of amides' pp. 113

- Proteins are hydrolysed into their constituent amino acids by heating with aqueous acid or alkali.
- This process is the reverse of the condensation polymerisation that forms proteins.
- This reaction is similar to that for the hydrolysis of amides.
- Biological systems use enzymes to catalyse this hydrolysis. This takes place at body temperature without the need for acid or alkali.

Fats and oils

Alkaline hydrolysis produces the carboxylate of the fatty acid

Fats are *triglyceryl esters* of fatty acids (long chain carboxylic acids) and propane-1,2,3–triol (glycerol).
Acid hydrolysis of each molecule produces:
- **three** fatty acid molecules, 3RCOOH and
- **one** molecule of glycerol (a triol), $HOCH_2CHOHCH_2OH$.

triglyceride *3 fatty acid molecules* *glycerol (propane-1,2,3-triol)*

Polymerisation

Properties
Polymers are:
- long-chain molecules with a high molecular mass
- made by joining together many small molecules called monomers.

Two types
- Addition polymerisation
- Condensation polymerisation

Addition polymerisation

- The monomer used is an unsaturated molecule containing a double C=C bond.
- The addition polymer formed is a saturated compound **without** double bonds.
- Many different addition polymers can be formed by using different monomer units.

Polyalkenes

You should be able to draw a short section of a polymer given the monomer units (and vice versa)

Make sure that you can show the repeat unit of a polymer

- Different alkene monomers produce different polymers.
- The double bond is lost as the polymer forms.
- The principle is the same for each addition polymerisation.
- The monomers are volatile liquids or gases.
- Polymers are solids.
- This difference in physical properties is explained by increased van der Waals' forces on polymerisation.

MONOMERS	→	POLYMER
unsaturated	→	saturated
Double bond	→	No double bond
n molecules	→	A **single** molecule

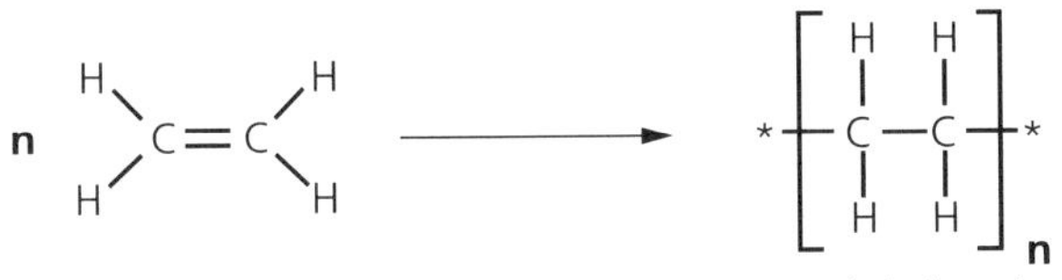

ethene → poly(ethene)

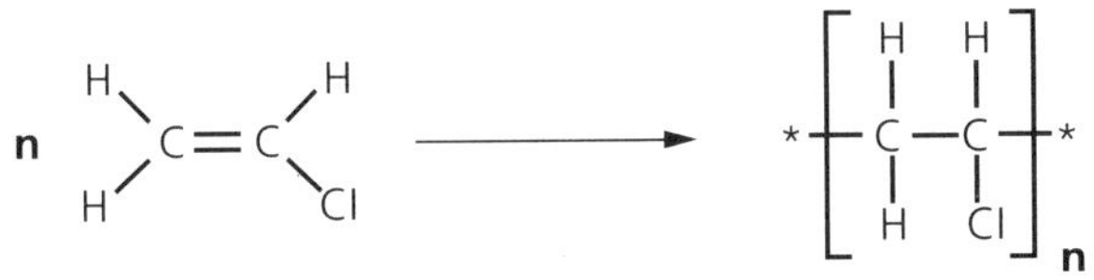

chloroethene → poly(chlorethene)

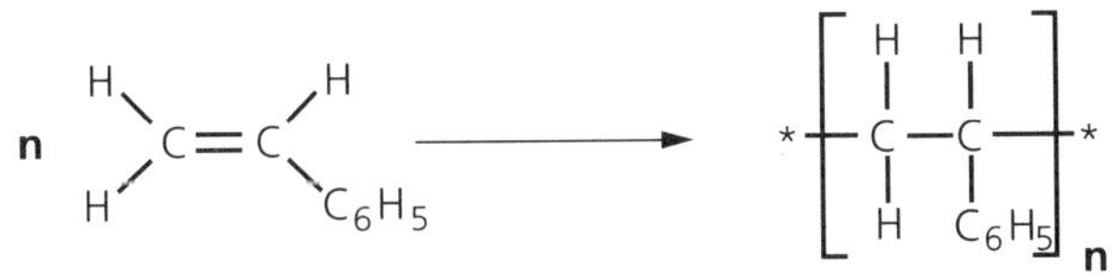

phenylethene → poly(phenylethene)

Problems with disposal

Polymers are non-biodegradable and take many years to break down.
Disposal by burning can produce toxic fumes (e.g. depolymerisation produces monomers; dioxins from combustion of chlorinated polymers).

Condensation polymerisation

- Two monomers are used for condensation polymerisation.
- Each bond that forms in the polymer also produces a small molecule such as H_2O or HCl.
- The common types are polyesters and polyamides.
- In the formation of the condensation polymer, two monomers A and B join alternately: –A–B–A–B–A–B–A–B–A–B–A–B–A–B–

Formation

In the reaction schemes below:
different polyesters and polyamides are made by using different ☐ units.

Polyesters

The monomers used are:
- a dicarboxylic acid
- a diol.

e.g. Terylene:
benzene-1,4-dicarboxylic acid

monomer A

ethane-1,2-diol

$$HO-\overset{\underset{H}{|}}{C}-\overset{\underset{H}{|}}{C}-OH$$

monomer B

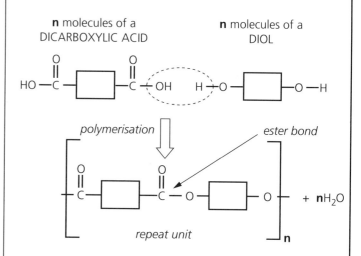

n molecules of a **DICARBOXYLIC ACID**   n molecules of a **DIOL**

polymerisation → *ester bond*

repeat unit   + nH_2O

A water molecule forms for each ester bond formed.

Polyamides

The monomers used are:
- a diacyl chloride
- a diamine.

e.g. Nylon 6,6

hexane-1,6-dioyl chloride

$$\overset{O}{\underset{Cl}{\diagdown}}C-(CH_2)_4-C\overset{O}{\diagup}_{Cl}$$

monomer A

1,6-diaminohexane
$$H_2N-(CH_2)_6-NH_2$$

monomer B

n molecules of a **DIACYL CHLORIDE**   n molecules of a **DIAMINE**

polymerisation → *amide bond*

repeat unit   + nHCl

A hydrogen chloride molecule forms for each amide bond formed.

Organic Synthetic Routes

- Summary charts are useful for showing the links between the functional groups. Questions are often set in exams asking for reagents, conditions or products.
- More searching problems may expect a synthetic route from a starting material to a final product. The synthetic route may include several stages.
- It is essential, if you are to answer such questions, that you thoroughly learn suitable reagents and conditions for all the reactions in your syllabus.

Aliphatic synthetic routes

The scheme below is based upon two main sets of reactions:
- a set based around bromoalkanes
- a set based around carboxylic acids and their derivatives.

The two sets of reactions are linked via the oxidation of primary alcohols.
- A reaction scheme based upon a secondary alcohol would result in oxidation to a ketone only.

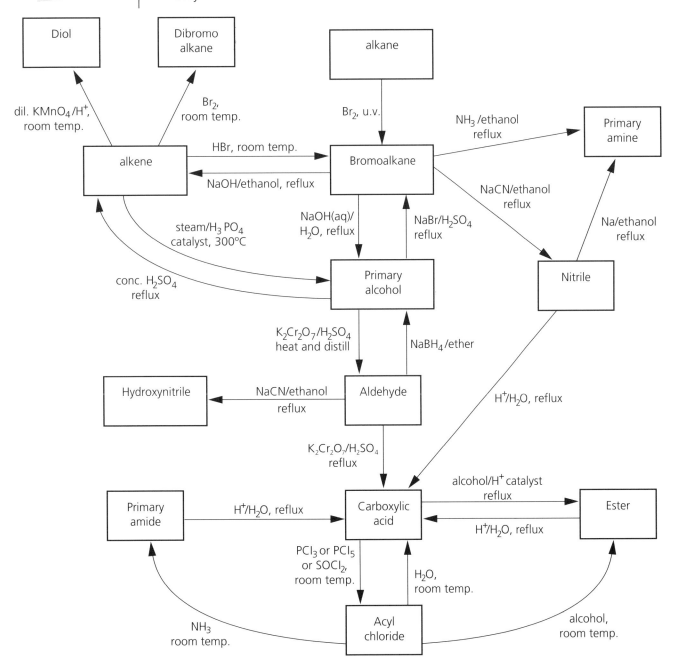

Aromatic synthetic routes

Compared with aliphatic organic chemistry at A-level, there are comparatively few aromatic reactions.

Benzene
- Reactions involving the benzene ring are mainly electrophilic substitution.

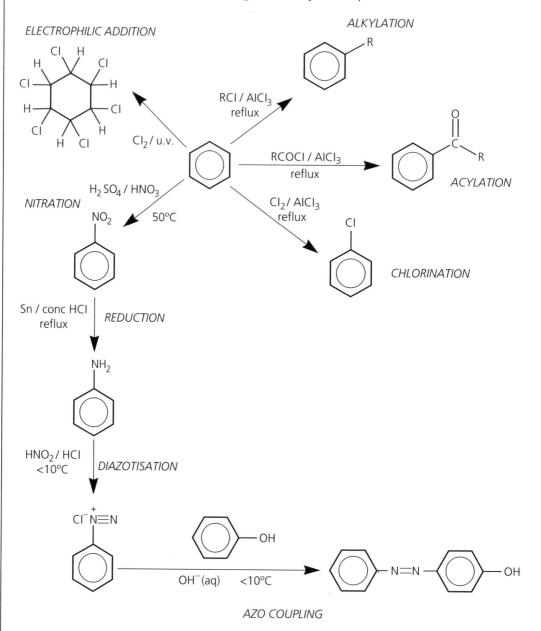

Methylbenzene
- More reactive and less vigorous conditions required.
- Main reactions are same but lead to 2- and 4-substituted products.
- Cl_2/u.v. results in substitution of side-chain.

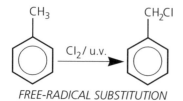

FREE-RADICAL SUBSTITUTION

Key reaction mechanisms

- Free-radical substitution
- Electrophilic addition
- Electrophilic substitution
- Nucleophilic substitution
- Nucleophilic addition

These mechanisms feature in most syllabuses although the examples required may differ – check

Free-radical substitution (see pp. 92):

see pp. 92

CL_2 and u.v. (methane and methylbenzene)

Initiation	Termination
$Cl_2 \longrightarrow 2\ Cl\bullet$	$Cl\bullet + Cl\bullet \longrightarrow Cl_2$
Propagation	$CH_3\bullet + Cl\bullet \longrightarrow CH_3Cl$
$CH_4 + Cl\bullet \longrightarrow CH_3\bullet + HCl$	$CH_3\bullet + CH_3\bullet \longrightarrow CH_3CH_3$
$CH_3\bullet + Cl_2 \longrightarrow CH_3Cl + Cl\bullet$	

Electrophilic addition (see pp. 93)

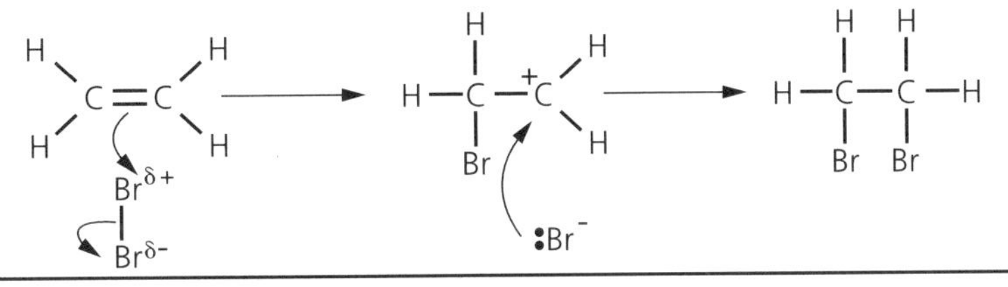

see pp. 93

alkenes and Br_2, HBr

Electrophilic substitution (see pp. 96)

see pp. 96

arenes and NO_2^+ and Cl_2

$$HNO_3 + H_2SO_4 \longrightarrow H_2NO_3^+ + HSO_4^-$$
$$H_2NO_3^+ \longrightarrow NO_2^+ + H_2O$$

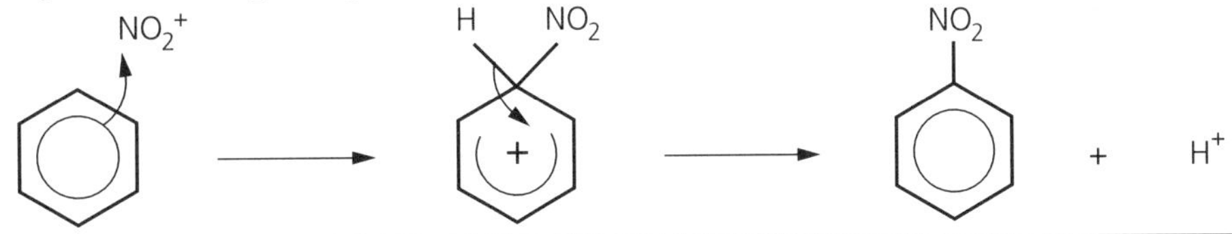

Nucleophilic substitution (see pp. 98)

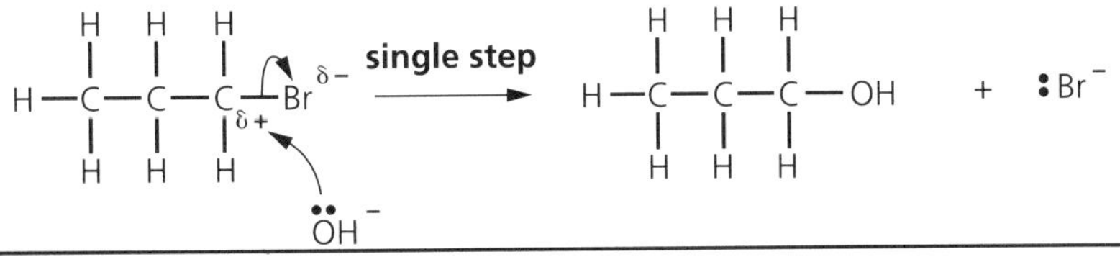

see pp. 98

RBr and OH^-, NH_3 and CN^-

Nucleophilic addition (see pp. 105)

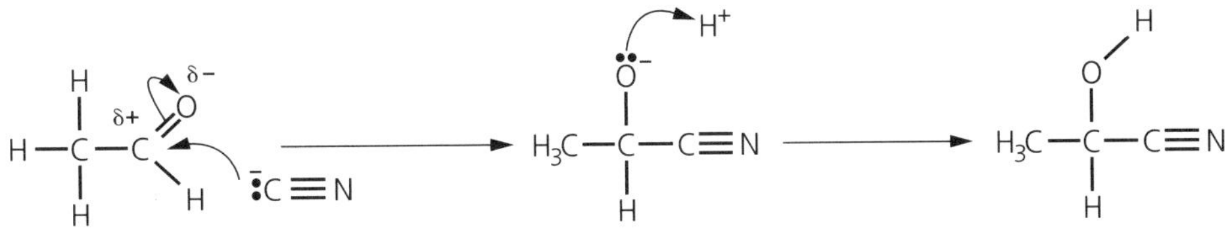

see pp. 105

carbonyl compounds and HCN

Check to see if you need to learn any more!

Other mechanisms

Some extra mechanisms that feature in syllabuses are shown below.

- Electrophilic addition of HBr and H_2SO_4 to unsymmetrical alkenes (e.g. propene).
- Nucleophilic addition-elimination reactions of acyl chlorides with H_2O, ROH, NH_3, RNH_2.
- Nucleophilic substitution of tertiary halogenoalkanes.
- Electrophilic substitution of arenes with RCl and RCOCl.
- Elimination of alcohols with H_2SO_4.

10 Spectra

Structural determination of organic compounds

Mass spectrometry

For spectra of organic molecules, the peaks of highest m/e are:
- the molecular ion peak, M, providing the molecular mass for molecules containing ^{12}C
- the M+1 peak showing the presence of ^{13}C

The M peak is formed by ionisation of a molecule following bombardment with electrons, *e.g., butanone, $CH_3COCH_2CH_3$:*

$$CH_3\overset{\overset{O}{\|}}{C}CH_2CH_3 + e^- \longrightarrow [CH_3\overset{\overset{O}{\|}}{C}CH_2CH_3]^+ + 2e^-$$

molecular ion,
m/e: 72

Fragmentation provides clues for the molecular structure of the compound,
e.g. **Fragmentation of $[CH_3COCH_2CH_3]^+$:**

- The most abundant peak in the mass spectrum is the base peak.
- The base peak in the mass spectrum of butanone has m/e: 43, formed by the loss of a $CH_3CH_2{}^\bullet$ free radical:

$$[CH_3\overset{\overset{O}{\|}}{C}CH_2CH_3]^+ \longrightarrow [CH_3\overset{\overset{O}{\|}}{C}]^+ \quad + \quad {}^\bullet CH_2CH_3$$

$\quad$ *molecular ion* $\qquad\qquad$ *fragment ion* $\qquad$ *free radical*
$\qquad$ *m/e: 72* $\qquad\qquad\qquad$ *m/e: 43* $\qquad\qquad$ *M−29*

- Different fragmentations are possible depending on the structure of the molecular ion.
- The fragment ions may themselves be fragmented further.

Mass spectrum of butanone, $CH_3COCH_2CH_3$

Like a jigsaw, the fragments can be reassembled to give the molecular structure.

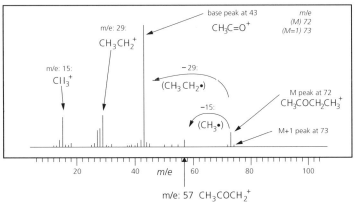

Common patterns in a mass spectrum

Common fragmentations	Common fragment ions
$CH_3{}^\bullet$ (−15)	$CH_3{}^+$ (m/e: 15)
$C_2H_5{}^\bullet$ (−29)	$C_2H_5{}^+$ (m/e: 29)
$C_3H_7{}^\bullet$ (−43)	$C_3H_7{}^+$ (m/e: 43)
$CH_3C=O^\bullet$ (−43)	$CH_3C=O^+$ (m/e: 43)
$C_6H_5{}^\bullet$ (−77)	$C_6H_5{}^+$ (m/e: 77)

See also Relative Atomic Masses from mass spectra pp. 5–6

The base peak is given a relative abundance of 100. Other peaks are compared with this base peak

A common mistake in exams is to show both the fragmentation products as ions

Note that only ions, $X^+(g)$, are detected in the mass spectrum. Uncharged species such as the free radical $Y{\bullet}(g)$ cannot be deflected within the mass spectrometer

Infra-red spectroscopy

Look for fragmentation patterns, especially these number patterns

- Certain bonds in a molecule absorb infra-red radiation at characteristic frequencies.
- This enables the identification of the functional groups present in a molecule.
- Most important for detection of C=O, O–H and, to a lesser extent, C–O.

You don't need to learn the absorption frequencies - the data are provided

Carbonyl compounds (aldehydes and ketones)
Butanone, $CH_3COCH_2CH_3$
- C=O absorption 1680 to 1750 cm^{-1}

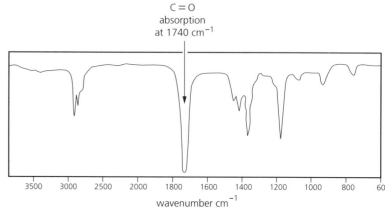

Alcohols
Ethanol, C_2H_5OH
- O–H absorption 3230 to 3500 cm^{-1}
- C–O absorption 1000 to 1300 cm^{-1}

Infra-red spectroscopy is most useful for identifying C=O and O-H bonds.
Look for the distinctive patterns

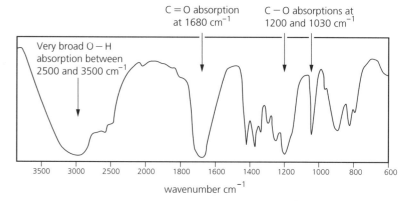

Carboxylic acids
Propanoic acid, C_2H_5COOH
- Very broad O–H absorption 2500 to 3500 cm^{-1}
- C=O absorption 1680 to 1750 cm^{-1}

Note that all these molecules contain C–H bonds which absorb in the range 2840 to 3045 cm^{-1}

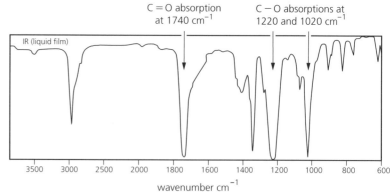

Ester
Ethyl ethanoate, $CH_3COOC_2H_5$
- C=O absorption 1680 to 1750 cm^{-1}
- C–O absorption 1000 to 1300 cm^{-1}

There are other organic groups (e.g. N–H, C=C) that absorb ir radiation but the principle of linking the group to the absorption wavenumber is the same

Fingerprint region

- Between 1000 and 1550 cm^{-1}
- Many spectra show a complex pattern of absorption in this range, unique for a particular compound. This can allow the compound to be identified by comparison of spectra.

Nuclear magnetic resonance

Key principles

- Nuclear magnetic resonance (n.m.r.) exploits the magnetic spin of the **nucleus** of an atom, not the electrons.
- Only nuclei with an odd number of nucleons (neutrons + protons) possess a magnetic spin, e.g. ^{1}H, ^{13}C. Proton n.m.r. spectroscopy is the most useful general purpose technique.
- Absorption of radio waves allows the nuclear spin to flip to a higher energy state in an applied magnetic field.
- Nuclear magnetic resonance occurs as protons resonate between their spin energy states.

The different nuclear spin states in an applied magnetic field

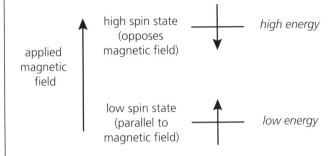

Chemical shift, δ

- The magnetic field at the nucleus of a particular proton is different to the applied magnetic field.
- Electrons around the nucleus *shield* the nucleus from the applied field. This difference is termed *nuclear shielding*.

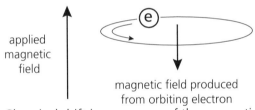

- Chemical shift is a measure of the magnetic field experienced by protons in different environments.

Typical chemical shifts

Extra shielding is provided by an electronegative atom or group.

- These are typical values.
- The actual chemical shift may be slightly different depending upon the actual environment.
- Note that the chemical shift for O–**H** can vary considerably and is dependent upon concentration, solvent and other factors.

type of proton	chemical shift, δ
R–C**H**$_3$;	0.9
R–C**H**$_2$–R	1.3
$\overset{O}{\overset{\|\|}{-C}}$–C**H**$_3$; $\overset{O}{\overset{\|\|}{-C}}$–C**H**$_2$–R	2.0
⬡—C**H**$_3$; ⬡—C**H**$_2$–R	2.3
X–C**H**$_3$; X–C**H**$_2$–R (X=halogen)	3.2–3.7
–O–C**H**$_3$; –O–C**H**$_2$–R	3.8
R–O–**H**	4.5
⬡—**H**	7

Margin notes:

The fingerprint region is unique for a particular compound

The energy gap is equal to that provided by radio waves

Protons in different environments absorb at different chemical shifts

Chemical shift, δ, is measured relative to a standard: tetramethylsilane (TMS), Si(CH$_3$)$_4$

You don't need to learn these – the data are provided

The only reliable means of identifying O–H in n.m.r. is to use D$_2$O: see Labile protons, pp. 120

N.m.r. spectra

A low resolution n.m.r. spectrum of ethanol has absorptions at three chemical shifts showing the three different environments:

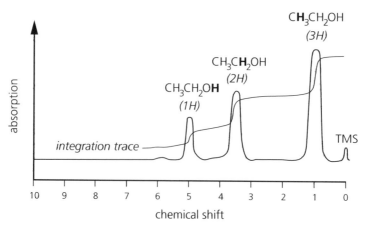

The area under each peak is in direct proportion to the number of protons responsible for the absorption.

Splitting patterns

- Neighbouring protons influence the magnetic field experienced by a proton.
- This can result in spin-spin coupling governed by the *n+1* rule:

> The number of peaks of a multiplet is equal to the number of equivalent **protons** in **neighbouring** atoms plus one.

- Equivalent protons do not interact with each other. The three equivalent CH_3 protons in ethanol cause splitting of the neighbouring CH_2 protons, not among themselves.

A high resolution n.m.r. spectrum of ethanol

Each main peak is itself split by neighbouring protons according to the *n+1* rule:

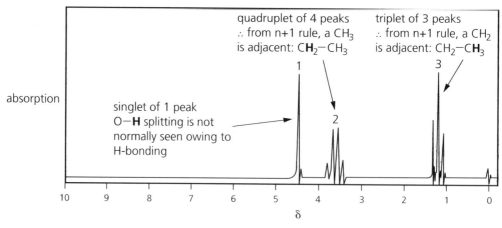

Labile protons

- The chemical shift at which O–H groups absorb is sensitive to solvents, substituents and concentration. This makes it difficult to identify O–H groups.
- A second n.m.r. spectrum is usually run with a small quantity of deuterium oxide, D_2O added.
- The D_2O exchanges with O–H protons and any such peak will disappear, thus allowing easy identification.

These pages are for your own notes.

Index